THE EXCELLENT 11

ALSO BY RON CLARK

The Essential 55
The Essential 55 Workbook

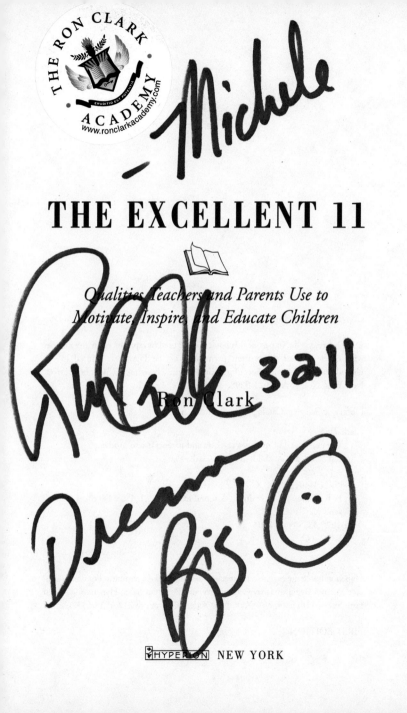

THE EXCELLENT 11

Qualities Teachers and Parents Use to Motivate, Inspire, and Educate Children

Ron Clark

HYPERION NEW YORK

— Michele

Ron Clark 3.2.11

Dream Big! ☺

Library of Congress Cataloging-in-Publication Data

Clark, Ron
     The excellent 11 : qualities teachers and parents use to motivate, inspire, and educate children / Ron Clark.
        p.   cm.
     ISBN 1-4013-0141-X
     1. Teaching.   2. Learning.   3. Conduct of life.   I. Title: Excellent eleven.   II. Title.
LB1025.3.C5344   2004
371.102—dc22

                                                               2004040641

Hyperion books are available for special promotions and premiums. For details contact Michael Rentas, Manager, Inventory and Premium Sales, Hyperion, 77 West 66th Street, 11th floor, New York, New York 10023, or call 212-456-0133.

FIRST EDITION

10   9   8   7   6   5

For all those who devote their lives
to placing passion and
a love of life
in the
hearts and minds
of others

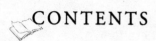

CONTENTS

INTRODUCTION

Mrs. owens scared the death out of me. She taught me biology, chemistry, and physics in high school, and those were three years I spent in complete fear of her wrath. Each day I would walk in Mrs. Owens's classroom to be met with her intense face, those piercing eyes hidden below her strong brow, and that gray hair swooping upward to give her already tall stature even more of an ominous presence. Yeah, I was scared.

Her appearance, however, was only the beginning. Mrs. Owens was the most demanding individual I have ever met. She would often declare in her bellowing voice, "I *insist* that you all succeed! Now *apply* yourself!" Her tests were brutal, and taking notes was a nightmare. I would have to run from my third period class to get to her room, and before I even made it and before the bell had rung, she would already be lecturing away. My classmates and I would be falling over one another to get in our seats and get started. Her room had chalkboards on all four walls, and she would fill up every inch of space on them, talking away all the while about grams, molecules, and weights. She would then pause, stand upright, look around, and finally say with intensity, "I need board space."

After all I went through during those three years, I was surprised to find that once I started teaching, I drew one very important lesson from Mrs. Owens: When you are dealing with children, above all else you must have passion. I learned more from Mrs. Owens than any other teacher I have ever had. When I got to college, all of my science courses were a breeze. As I took my exams, I could see Mrs. Owens standing over me and lecturing about everything from electrons to protoplasm. Her passion and enthusiasm for her subjects were infectious, and we all worked three times as hard in her class as we did in the others. I remember one time when Mrs. Owens was having problems with her back. She came to school on a stretcher (no exaggeration) and, lying flat on her back, wheeled herself around the room from chalkboard to chalkboard. She claimed she would let nothing short of death come between her students and their education.

As I started to teach, I tried to carry that fire and determination with me as well. I attempted, however, to temper that drive with another very important component: compassion. I can remember my first day of kindergarten. I was crying and didn't want Mom to leave, and Mrs. Clark, my teacher, was trying her best to calm me down. Mrs. Clark was an elderly lady with a kind face, gentle hands, and warm spirit. She looked down and told me that my shoes were untied, and I told her I didn't know how to tie them. She just smiled and said, "Now that won't do, will it?" She started helping me tie my shoes, and after a few minutes she said, "You see, you can tie your shoes, and that's only one of the many things you will learn this year." I looked up, my eyes dry, and saw that Mom was gone. She had slipped out and allowed me to take that step on my own. She later told me that she sat in the parking lot and cried for an hour, but I am glad she didn't come back in. Mrs. Clark's kindness and sweet voice had won me over, and I felt safe and loved in her classroom.

As I look back over my time as a student, there were so many wonderful qualities shared by my teachers. I can remember loving the spark of energy that I experienced every day in Mrs. Roach's second grade class. It was one adventure after the next, and I loved never knowing what to expect. I told her one day how my favorite song was "Funky Town," and I asked her if I could bring it in to share with the class. I was shocked to hear her say, "Only if you will dance with me in front of everyone and show them how to get funky." I agreed, and the next day we danced and danced and laughed until we both fell on the floor.

The best teachers I ever had, my parents, taught me more about qualities that are needed when dealing with children than anyone I've ever known. They always took the time to remind me of the importance and lasting effects of showing appreciation, the value of common sense, and the need for humor and laughter in the lives of us all. They are so loving and dear to me, and I can never thank them enough for the sacrifices they made for me and their dedication in trying to raise me in the best possible way.

This past year I have had the opportunity to travel all over the country, to leave my classroom and enter those of others, to speak to teachers and parents, and to learn about education in America. It has been a wonderful and magnificent journey that I wouldn't trade for anything in the world. On my travels to schools and districts in forty-nine states I have met numerous people who also possess the special qualities shared by many of my teachers and my parents. After meeting so many exceptional individuals I decided to compile a list of the eleven qualities that seem to be present in all exceptional teachers, parents, and students. These are the qualities that I have seen others display and are also the ones that I discovered were necessary for me to become the best teacher I felt I could possibly be.

I hope this serves as a guide to you and assists you not only as you display these qualities yourself but also as you attempt to impart them to the hearts and minds of your children and students.

THE EXCELLENT 11

 1. ENTHUSIASM

*Your enthusiasm will be infectious, stimulating,
and attractive to others. They will love you for it.
They will go for you and with you.*

—NORMAN VINCENT PEALE (1898–1993)

I LIST THIS QUALITY first for a reason. Nothing is more important than having enthusiasm. If you are a teacher, the students will be excited about learning a lesson if you are eager and excited about teaching it. If you are a parent, children will care about things if they see that they mean a lot to you and that you are energized by them. Children are impressionable, and when they look to adults for guidance, we must inspire them and motivate them to want to learn, to have a desire to achieve, and to want to be the best person they can be.

Enthusiasm Is Contagious

The end-of-grade test scores are looked at very closely in North Carolina. At the end of one school year our faculty and staff were all nervous about hearing whether our school would be designated "low-performing," just "met growth," or was an "exemplary school." We were in a financially disadvantaged area and always felt that we were playing catch-up with our students, trying our best to get them on grade level. Some years we saw outstanding growth, but the students, no matter how far they came, didn't score on level. It was frustrating and demoralizing for all the teachers. Some individual teachers would get wonderful results with their students, but we didn't seem able to pull it all together as a school. In my fourth year at Snowden Elementary, however, the entire school was named an "exemplary school." It was a huge boost to the teachers and staff, and we were all so excited that we wanted to do something to show the students how much their achievements meant to us. The ideas we came up with cost money, and since it was the end of the year, none of our plans seemed possible on such short notice. A group of us started talking about how neat it would be to have a teacher talent show as a salute to the students. We would dress up as our favorite musical stars from the sixties, seventies, eighties, or nineties and lip-sync before the entire body of students from pre-kindergarten through the eighth grade. I have this thing about surprises, so we agreed that we wouldn't tell the students what was going on; we would just take them to the gym-atorium one day and give them a huge shock!

Our idea was great, but there was a problem: Many

teachers didn't want to do it. They felt the students would lose respect for them and they would look foolish. They said it was too much work, they didn't have a costume or know the words to any songs, and they had no time to practice. In addition, if all the teachers were backstage, there would be no one to watch the students. There was a great deal of pessimism and a lack of morale. On the other hand, the small group of teachers I was working with was enthusiastic and excited about the show, and they kept at it, encouraging other teachers, helping them find costumes, and getting the music together.

One teacher, Mrs. Bagalour, was very negative. She wasn't one of the students' favorite teachers, because she basically just sat at her desk all day, earning the students' nickname for her of "Mrs. Bag-of-flour." She said there was no way she was getting on the stage, but I knew the kids would love it if she participated. A small group of teachers was going to perform "Charlie Brown," and I suggested to Mrs. Bagalour that she sit at a desk, play the part of a student, and throw paper at the teacher along with the other "students." It took a lot of persuading, but she finally agreed.

Slowly but surely the enthusiastic teachers started to spread their energy around to the other faculty members. We reminded everyone what the show was for and told them how much it would affect the students. We showed them how excited we were about the show and put a little pressure on them to take part. As they heard about the great ideas others had and the effort they were putting into their performance, some of them wanted to become part of the show. As everyone was getting involved and everyone became more excited, no one wanted to be left out.

There was one last obstacle: A teacher named Mrs. Brokard said she wasn't going to perform because she wanted a certain rendition of the song she was singing, "Ain't No Mountain High Enough," and no one could find it. She said she knew all the words to it, and if that rendition was found, she would put on the show of a lifetime. If it wasn't found, she would not participate. Good grief, the drama. Luckily, my dad used to be a disc jockey in the seventies, and I found myself looking through boxes and boxes of his old albums. When I finally found that song, I felt as if I had actually climbed a mountain myself. I walked in the next morning and showed the record to Mrs. Brokard. She looked a little shocked, a little scared, and a little worried, but she also looked a little excited.

Soon the day came for the show. As with any school, word had spread that something was going on, but the students couldn't figure out what it was. The students had caught a few glimpses during the week: a feather boa sticking out of Mrs. Woolard's car trunk; teachers passing cassette tapes back and forth; Mrs. Wilson staring into space while bobbing her head and making short movements with her feet; and everyone on the faculty walking with a bit of spirit and excitement. We told our students at lunchtime that they would be going to the gym later for a surprise but that any misbehavior whatsoever would ruin it for everyone. Parents and substitutes watched our classes while we transformed ourselves behind the stage. Soon the extravaganza began. When the curtain opened, the students were informed that they were about to witness a presentation in their honor for their outstanding efforts that year. They were told it was a gift from the teachers because they appreciated each and every one of them and that they were doing this because they cared for all the students of Snowden. And then came the magic. Teachers who never seemed to show enthusiasm or spark were standing before the students, dressed to the nines, dancing and singing away. Mrs. Sawyer was transformed into Diana Ross. Mrs. Jones shocked everyone as Olivia Newton-John from *Grease*. Mrs. Zurface joined with three others to form the Spice Girls, a crowd favorite. And Mrs. Brokard walked out to cheers as she sang "Ain't No Mountain High Enough." You know, after all that effort, she didn't really know all the words, but she sure put on a show, grinning from ear to ear and working that song. The kids absolutely loved it, and their behavior was perfect—clapping loudly, paying attention, and showing respectful gratitude with several standing ovations.

Something was different about our school after that day. We were all a little closer, everyone seemed much happier, and our discipline problems went down drastically. Some said that the students wouldn't respect them if they sang and danced like that, but, on the contrary, they seemed to respect and appreciate us a lot more.

Enthusiasm is a powerful thing, and it is contagious. When you can use energy, excitement, and a spark to motivate others, you are affecting more people than you can ever know. Those students in Aurora still talk about that show we put on. They say they will never forget it. Whether you are a parent or a teacher, use your enthusiasm to motivate others and affect as many kids as possible. Don't take no for an answer, and when you come across those individuals who stand in your way, do whatever it takes to climb that mountain and take them with you.

✐Enthusiasm Is Best When It Serves a Purpose

It's one thing to have a lot of enthusiasm and energy, and it's another thing to use that spirit and attitude to make a difference. When I was teaching in North Carolina, there was a young teacher named Mrs. Bodler who was extremely motivated. She wanted to be the best teacher she could be, and every day she was practically bouncing off the walls in her classroom, dressing up as characters and bringing in all types of props and colorful games. There was a problem, though. She was doing a lot more "rah-rah" and cheering than actually addressing the educational needs of her students, and soon she voiced her concern to me that her students weren't doing well on any of their tests. Usually when that happens to me, I ask myself two questions: Did the test adequately measure the material I taught the students? Did I do a good job of teaching the material? In Mrs. Bodler's case the problem always seemed to be with the latter of the two. She just wasn't doing a good job of teaching her students, no matter how much energy she was putting into her lessons. It was as if she was spinning her wheels.

In my classroom I spend a lot of time rapping lessons, dancing, jumping on desks, standing on my head, and doing whatever it takes to get my students excited and enthusiastic about learning. I have to remind myself constantly, however, that I must focus on the educational purpose behind my antics, and I have to make sure that everything I do is not only motivating my students but also meeting their challenges and helping them learn the concepts I am trying to teach. The first year I taught, I decided to give my students a challenge. I told them that I expected them to memorize the names of all forty-two presidents in order. They had to stand at the front of the classroom and say the names, giving facts about each president and each first lady along the way. This may be hard to understand, but I wanted those students to have a sense of accomplishment, something they could "touch." Most of the students in that class had such low self-esteem and seemed to have already given up. I wanted them to accomplish something *big,* something *great,* so that they would have pride in their achievement. I also had an educational purpose, because I was having the hardest time teaching my students American history. They, like most ten-year-olds, didn't have any concept of when events actually occurred in history and how long ago fifty years was as opposed to three hundred years.

Before I decided to have them memorize the presidents, I tried using a timeline that stretched across the front of the room. It listed all the major events in the United States from the American Revolution to the present. Each day during our lessons I would point out such things as the shot heard around the world, Orville and Wilbur's flight, Martin Luther King, Jr.'s assassination, and other major events. As I moved from one side of the class to the other, pointing out key points and discussing the relationships between events, I was sure the students were really going to grasp an understanding of the course of events in our country, but, unfortunately, it didn't work nearly as well as I had hoped. The students still couldn't pull it all together and see the "big picture." That is when I decided to have my students memorize all the presidents' names. That is the one theme you can track from day one in our country until now. I figured that if they knew all the presidents and could associate the major events of each term with the person who was president, it would help them understand and remember the things I had outlined on the timeline.

When I first told the class what I expected of them, they were all shocked and said it was impossible. That is the response I wanted. I wanted those kids to consider it an insurmountable task; that way, when they accomplished it, the pride they felt would be that much greater. I then told them that I would be giving only two grades for the assignments, one hundred or zero. I told them that even if they said forty-one presidents, forgetting only one, they would receive a zero. It sounds harsh, and I know it. I just didn't want the students to think there was any doubt whatsoever that they could know the name of every single president from memory. I believe that as teachers we must set the bar as high as possible. I am a firm believer that we can get out of students what we expect, and if we aren't setting our expectations extremely high, students aren't going to perform extremely high.

After the assignment was given, I used every tactic I could think of to motivate the students. I learned the presidents myself, reciting them with pride in front of the students and showing them that it was possible. I acted as if I felt like the king of the world because I could say all the presidents. I then made up a rap song about the presidents, singing it during recess and at lunch, getting the students excited. As I taught history, I would impersonate different presidents and tell the students unique and interesting stories about their times in office. I tried to place a relationship in their minds between the man as president and the events that were going on during his presidency. Nothing fosters effort more than unity, so I divided the students into teams of seven. I taught sixty-three students throughout the day, so we had nine teams. I then recruited a faculty member to be on each team. If every person on each team could say the presidents in order by the end of the month, that team would get a free pizza party. The pressure was on! Students were quizzing each other, stopping their faculty team member in the hallway, supporting one another, practicing, calling one another on the phone, and putting forth much effort to learn the presidents. It was wonderful, fun, and exciting! As different students finally learned them all, they would recite them with pride, holding their heads high and smiling from ear to ear.

The final day of the month soon arrived, and every single child stood in front of the class, naming each president to the cheers and applause of all their classmates. There were different learning levels in my classes and several of the students had learning disabilities, but each and every child accomplished the task, saying every president from memory without missing a single name. I have never seen students so proud of themselves. It was a wonderful occasion.

We went to the local pizza restaurant to have our party, and every waitress had to hear each kid recite all the presidents. For the rest of that year, no matter where we went or whom we met, they *had* to hear those presidents. The kids were proud, and they all felt a sense of accomplishment. The best part, however, is that teaching history became so much easier. The students were far more interested; they were able to make connections to events that occurred and truly develop an understanding of American history. To this day when I see those students, they can still recite the presidents, and many of them can still sing the president rap song. I've included a copy of the song in the appendix for any parents or teachers who might be interested in sharing it with your own children.

A lot of time, effort, and energy went into making the project of learning the presidents work, but the outcome made it all worth it. Teachers should always clearly outline their objectives and set educational goals that are challenging and beneficial. They should then light a fire that will spark each and every child to reach those goals and attain the desired knowledge.

✎ Enthusiasm Is Fueled by Our Surroundings

In one year's time a teacher can spend nearly a quarter of the entire year in his or her classroom. That is an incredible amount of time to spend in one place, and we should do whatever it takes to make that room a place where we are comfortable, inspired, and enthusiastic about teaching. I recently visited the classroom of a friend of mine, Kim Stewart, and I couldn't believe it! It looked like something out of *Better Homes and Gardens*. The walls were painted purple and green; there was a couch, flowers, pictures in frames, a mirror on the wall, and carpet on the floor. This fits Kim's personality, and I could tell she felt a lot of ownership and pride in her room. She told me that she wanted to feel comfortable in her surroundings, because she knew she would do a better job of teaching and her students would enjoy learning more if they were in a pleasing atmosphere.

This is hard for a lot of teachers to accomplish, because they don't know if they will be in the same room the following year or there might be restrictions about what can be done to certain rooms. Some teachers are allowed to paint walls only if they agree to repaint the walls their original color at their own expense. Some principals don't even want to hear the word *paint*. My first year teaching, I really wanted to do something special with my room. It was such a dull room, full of brown and gray, and it seemed to smell like chalk and musk with a hint of Raid. I hated it, and I knew my students would as well. I drove to town and bought eight gallons of electric blue paint #9. I decided it would be best not to ask permission, and I just started painting everything—the cabinets, the walls, the shelves, everything! When I was done, it looked great, but in the middle of the room sat thirty-four old, rusty metal desks. Some were brown, some green, some yellow, and they were all different sizes. These desks were the leftovers from other grades. I knew that I could repaint the walls white, if they threatened to fire me, but if I painted those desks, there was no turning back. I stood there for a few minutes, and then I slowly touched the end of the brush to the bottom of the seat, electric blue exploding across the dull yellow. It looked good. I painted every desk.

After days of working with my door shut, I was ready to get the principal. It was my moment of reckoning. As we walked into the room, Mrs. Roberson stepped back, a look of horror on her face. I was talking as fast as I could: "I can repaint it at the end of the year and the kids will love it and I know how you talk so much about getting the kids excited about learning and this room was so boring and those seats are so old anyway and this way you won't have to order new desks for years and I really think it looks so much better. . . ." She stood there for a minute, and then she said, "Mr. Clark, you are going to be the death of me." But I could tell by her tone that she wasn't really angry. I do think she believed I would shorten her days on earth, though.

When the kids walked in on the first day of school, you would have thought they were walking into Disneyland. Their mouths dropped as they looked around at the bright colors. They loved it, and from the first moment I could tell they all wanted to be in that class. And I did as well.

As I said, painting a room or making permanent changes to a classroom isn't going to fly in a lot of schools, but there are things that can be done to make it a more enjoyable place to be in. Teachers can place pictures of family and friends on their desks; put construction paper over the door or cover an entire wall with it and decorate that; put up interesting posters; use one's favorite colors and make the room bright and cheerful; and put a plant in the room. I think every room should have a plant somewhere; it just gives the room a totally different feel.

For parents or teachers who tutor kids, it's important that the environment where they are being tutored or doing their homework is one they will enjoy. Make sure the seat is comfortable and that there is plenty of light and not too much clutter around. Make sure there is a dictionary nearby, along with pens, pencils, a sharpener, a ruler, tape, and a calculator. Having an area set up where learning, studying, and homework are easier and more enjoyable will help kids become more enthusiastic about getting to work and completing assigned tasks.

✎ Placing Enthusiasm In the Hearts of Unmotivated Children

Children get excited and enthusiastic about learning when they are confident, see they can be successful, are having fun, and are praised. Those four components will light a fire in the hearts of students and get them to perform. With every lesson I teach, I make sure to start off by covering those four components. I might say to the class, "I know you are going to do really well at this," to build up confidence. I take it in steps and review as I go so that the students feel successful along the way. I let them know I am enjoying the lesson, and

I try to make it fun for them. And, finally, I praise the class as a whole and individuals as often as possible. Even using those strategies, there always seem to be a few students in every class who are impossible to reach. They aren't interested, are usually below grade level, and tend to be discipline problems. Figuring out ways to reach them is an enormous challenge. I found that sometimes I spent so much time trying to reach those few that the rest of the class was suffering. At what point do you abandon the efforts to reach the stubborn few in order to meet the needs of the rest of the class? For me that is always hard, because the more troubled a student seems, the more I want to help.

There was a student I taught in New York City named Emanuel. He hadn't seen his parents for years and was living with a family member who didn't seem thrilled to be responsible for him. When I visited the home before the first day of school, Emanuel's uncle sat beside him on the couch and said things like "This boy is nothing but trouble, and you are going to have your hands full this year. He barely passed the fourth grade, and I don't see why they didn't hold him back." As he talked, I just watched Emanuel put his head down and avoid looking me in the eye. I decided that I was going to do whatever it took to reach Emanuel that year. I was going to change his life and get him to reach his potential.

As the school year progressed, I realized my task wasn't going to be easy. Emanuel would never do his homework, and he didn't care if I gave him silent lunch or detention.

He made fun of the other kids and was the source of conflict every time I turned around. He had so much anger in him that he would barely calm down to listen when I tried to reason with him. One day as school started I looked up and saw his seat empty, and I'm embarrassed to admit it, but I was actually glad. A day without Emanuel was going to be so much easier. Five minutes later, however, he walked in. Why is it that the students who present the most discipline challenges always have perfect attendance? As Emanuel went to his seat, I just felt sick. I had actually hoped he wouldn't show up. How could I feel that way? I realized I had to change my relationship with Emanuel.

I started making visits to his home to help with his homework. I moved his desk to the front row in the center. I stayed after school with him and let him help me set up the classroom for the following day. I praised him and made sure to call on him as often as I could during my lessons. I was putting forth a great deal of effort, but his behavior barely changed. He was still bothering others, causing chaos on the playground, not doing all his work, and not even trying academically. In return for the marginal improvements I saw, I was depriving the rest of the class, who also had their share of challenges, of my attention and effort. I finally realized I had to stop spending so much time focusing on Emanuel, because the rest of the class was suffering. In a way I feel I gave up on him. I still worked to contain his behavior and still tried to get him to focus, but for the most part I had to limit my time so that I could address the needs of the class as a whole. At the end of the year the class's test scores were extremely high, but Emanuel's were at the very bottom. I was going to teach the sixth grade the following year, and I asked the principal if I could have Emanuel in my class again. I felt as though I had failed him, and I wanted another chance. She agreed, but that summer Emanuel moved and I never saw him again.

Did I handle the situation the correct way? I don't know. I know I felt horrible about it, and I have since spent a lot of time thinking about Emanuel and how I could have handled the situation differently. I know that if I were the parent of a fifth grade child, I would dislike a teacher's spending a great deal of time on one student and essentially ignoring the needs of my child and the others in the class. Yet I still have that desire to reach the ones who are the most troubled, and I constantly struggle with how to manage that while also addressing the needs of the other students.

I had another student named Nykal whose situation was very similar to Emanuel's. He also was a major discipline problem and was carrying a lot of baggage from his home life and his experiences on the streets. He didn't seem to respect anything I said, and even though he was in the sixth grade, he acted as if he was eighteen years old. One of his main problems was that he struggled in every subject and had very little self-esteem. I came up with a plan. I took Nykal and three of the brightest students out into the hall and told them that the superintendent wanted to reward four students who I felt had the most potential in the classroom and that I had picked them to receive the honor. The three brightest students, all girls, just beamed, but Nykal looked stunned. I sent home letters to their parents, and that Friday after school, I took the kids out for pizza. We laughed and talked and had a great bonding experience. We then headed to the board of education. I had mailed four certificates to the superintendent and discussed with him what I was doing, and how he was to present the certificates to the students upon our arrival. We reached the office and the superintendent went on and on about how proud he was of the students and gave them their certificates. Those students were just as happy as if the president himself had given them the awards. I didn't know if my tactic was going to work, but I could tell by the look on Nykal's face that he was happy and that it meant something to him that I had selected him as a student of "great potential." The next day when Nykal walked in the class he said, "What's up, Mr. Clark," and there was respect and appreciation in his voice. That entire day he focused, took notes, and tried his best.

Nykal is a success story. He continued to try harder and was soon performing much better in the classroom. With a little extra attention his behavior problems were greatly reduced, and he seemed to be a much happier child. Getting him enthusiastic about learning took building his confidence and making him feel that he had the potential to succeed. Putting forth the extra effort in his case worked.

So at what point do we sacrifice the good of the entire class to devote more attention to getting a few unmotivated students enthusiastic about learning? That has to be left up to the individual teacher. In my opinion, however, too often not enough effort is being placed on reaching those challenging students, and teachers give up on them too quickly. For every Emanuel out there, there are a dozen Nykals that can be reached by the influence and impact of a caring role model. It's my hope that in every classroom out there teachers will work with passion, energy, and enthusiasm, but at the same time I hope that all teachers will provide a little extra attention, compassion, and confidence building to those students who are struggling and so often fall between the cracks.

Effects of Enthusiasm on Others

I did my student teaching with eleventh graders. I will never forget the first day of my ten-week assignment at the school. As student teachers we were supposed to observe for a number of days before picking up one of the classes, and then we would progressively pick up others until the final two weeks when we would be responsible for teaching all five classes. I walked into the classroom and talked with my cooperating teacher. After five minutes he said, "Well, Ron, you seem to have your head on your shoulders. Why don't you go ahead and pick up all five classes starting tomorrow?" I was wide-eyed and had no idea what it meant to be a teacher, and I just said, "Okay." The next day I stood in front of the first period class, and for the first few minutes my eyes started to water and I found myself having to swallow a lot. The class was well behaved, and the students seemed to be encouraging me, smiling and nodding their heads as I talked. To mask my fear and uneasiness, I just started throwing myself into it. I was moving my arms as I talked, walking from side to side. I remember my mother telling me that if I ever had to speak in front of people, I should use props and have things to point at. She said that when you are pointing at things, everyone will look there, and it will take the pressure off you. So I drew on the board a lot and pulled down maps and hopped around. All in all, it was a great class. As the day wore on, I realized that all the students were not going to be quite like that first period. They seemed to get progressively worse, and by the time the sixth period class walked in, I was afraid to even look. The twenty-one students in the class had all failed U.S. history previously, and it was obvious that none of them cared if they failed it again. As they came in, one guy walked up to me, made his hand into a gun, put it in my face, and said in a calm and eerie voice, "Boom." I was downright terrified.

As I started "teaching" the class, none of the students were looking at me, half of them were talking, and one guy who was sitting by the window opened it up and crawled out. I started calling to him, but the other students just said, "He does that all the time. His car's right out there." I had no idea how to get these kids to want to be there or to care, but I did what my instincts told me to do: I threw myself into the lesson, using enthusiasm and showing the students that I was excited about what I was teaching them. I mentioned several times how they had to pass U.S. history in order to graduate and that I wanted to help them do that. I told them that I wanted to see all of them walk across the stage on graduation day, and I said something like "I know you aren't interested in what I have to teach you, but if we work together, it can be fun and easy, and you can all get that diploma." They weren't convinced, but I still continued to use enthusiasm in every lesson, and slowly I started to notice something. The students in sixth period started to work harder, and it didn't seem to have anything to do with graduation or grades; they were working harder because they wanted to please me and make me proud. They saw how enthusiastic I was about teaching, and I think that meant something to them; in turn, they started to perform. Over the final five weeks of my student teaching, those kids put forth a great amount of effort, and sixth period became my favorite time of the day. When my final day arrived, the students brought a balloon and a card they had all signed. It read, "Thank you for believing in us." A balloon and a card might not seem like much, but coming from the kids in that class, it meant the world to me.

There are numerous techniques to get kids to perform,

but none is more effective than simply being enthusiastic yourself. When you show that you really care about something and that it means a lot to you, even the most challenging of individuals will tend to get on board and help achieve the goal you have in mind.

When we are active and truly enthusiastic about our lives and jobs, we are often much happier. When individuals don't enjoy their jobs or aren't pleased with some facet of their life, they tend to have less energy; they gain weight, can't get sound sleep, and experience lethargy. When we engage in activities we enjoy and have an occupation that excites us, we feel better about ourselves, have greater self-esteem, wake up energized, laugh a lot more, and live longer. Having enthusiasm in our lives can be self-sustaining and affect our outlook more than we realize.

One thing I always tell my students is "Be the master of your own destiny." I want them to realize that as they go through life, they will have choices, and it is crucial that they choose to go down the roads that will fill their lives with excitement, service to others, laughter, and activities they can be enthusiastic about.

2. ADVENTURE

Only those who will risk going too far can possibly find out how far one can go.

—ABRAHAM LINCOLN (1809–1865)

T OO MANY STUDENTS ARE sitting in classrooms day after day, watching the clock and feeling bored. These same students at home are sitting on the couch and staring at the TV. As parents and teachers we must find a way to get these students motivated and excited about something in their lives. We have to place a spark in their hearts and give them something to look forward to. By creating an adventure for children we are not only teaching them a great deal but are also building their confidence, fostering trust, and encouraging them to become better students.

✐ Teachers and Parents Should Often Call Upon Their Youthful Sense of Adventure

I once took ten of my students from Harlem on a field trip to North Carolina. One of the girls in the class had put in her end-of-the-year scrapbook that her main dream in life would be to travel to North Carolina to see all the things Mr. Clark had talked about all year and to experience life as he explained it in his memories of home. I knew right then I would take her, along with as many other kids as I could manage. While on the trip we visited the sand dunes at Nags Head. These are humongous mountains of sand that reach high above the ocean and seem to touch the clouds. As a boy I used to climb all the way to the top with my sister, Tassie, and then roll down at the speed of light. I told my students how much fun it would be, but they only said they were not interested in ruining their clothes, getting sand in their sneakers or hair, or looking stupid as they rolled down the hill. These city kids from Harlem seemed desperate for a taste of something different from the streets where they grew up, but they weren't quite ready to let go.

The students did agree, however, to climb to the top of the largest sand dune with me. Once we were at the top, I looked over at Derrick, and I could see the wheels turning in his head. He said quietly and in a way that let me know he wasn't too sure of himself: "Mr. Clark . . . ah, I will roll down this mountain if you will." All of the other kids started to clamor and doubt his claim, but I only said, "Okay, Derrick, let's do it." We walked to the edge and looked over. The sand dunes don't have an extremely steep incline, but, still, I *am* afraid of heights, and the thought of rolling down the hill in my thirties carried much more fear than I remembered having as a boy.

We stepped to the edge, however, and after one look, we were off, rolling and rolling. I could barely keep my eyes open as sand and air flew across my face. I could hear Derrick yelling and laughing, over and over and over, and then suddenly we stopped. I looked over at Derrick, who was lying about ten feet from me. His chest was heaving, and he had the biggest grin on his face. He exclaimed, "Mr. Clark, that is the most fun I have ever had in my life!" Then I heard screams, and to my shock I looked up to see the other nine students flying down the dune, twists of arms, legs, sneakers, and braids in clouds of sand and dust, rolling and laughing at the speed of light. When they all landed, there was sand everywhere—all over their faces, in their mouths, throughout their hair weaves, inside ruined $100 sneakers, and covering every inch of their bodies. They just laughed. We all laughed, holding our sides, catching our breath, and getting ready to climb up the mountain of sand so that we could do it all again.

That was an experience those kids will never forget for the rest of their lives. They let so much go on that mountain: bad memories, stress, fear, appearances. All were gone. They just were living for the moment, and they were free.

Life can be really difficult for teenagers, and they are often so worried about what others will think that they won't let down their guard. As teachers and parents we need to make sure they are in an environment where they feel that they can be themselves, laugh, and be free. The best way teachers and parents can do this is to lead by example and be willing to call upon their own youthful sense of adventure when needed. I was not too keen on rolling down that sand dune in my dress pants and shirt, but I knew it was one of those times when I just needed to meet the challenge and show my students how much fun it can be to take a risk and experience life.

Teachers can apply that attitude in the classroom in many different ways. It can be done with something as simple as dressing up during Homecoming Week. Many schools have special days when the students are allowed to dress up, such as Twin Day, Sixties Day, School Spirit Day, or Backwards Day, when clothes are supposed to be worn inside out. I can remember when I was in school and some teachers would participate and others wouldn't. One thing is for sure: The students definitely notice those who are willing to join in and those who choose not to be part of the festivities. It seems like such an insignificant thing to add a little flavor to your attire for a few days, but it is something that the students all talk about, and they appreciate the showing of school spirit. In addition, if the students see how much fun you have with your costume, then it may encourage them to dress up as well on the following days.

I remember one time at Snowden Elementary when I was walking down the hall and heard music coming from Ms. Moore's second grade classroom. They were learning about different cultures around the world and the different ways they celebrated. At this point they were learning about the limbo, and Ms. Moore and Mrs. Dudley, her assistant, had set up a stick going across two desks. The students were just walking slowly, bending backward, and not really giving it a lot of effort. I walked in and said, "Oh, my goodness! I love to limbo!" I jumped in line, and when it came time to go under the stick, I started dancing and moving and acting as if I was really getting into it. After I had passed completely under without falling, Ms. Moore started laughing and said, "Mr. Clark, you are just plain crazy!" I grabbed her and Mrs. Dudley and said, "Oh, no, you're not getting away without doing this," and I pulled them into the line. They laughed and squealed and said there was no way they were doing it, but the kids started clapping and cheering and urging them on. Eventually they both made their way under the limbo stick to the enjoyment of every child in that classroom and of the teachers themselves.

Sometimes as teachers we have to remember what it feels like to be young and to re-create that sense of daring. We have to take a few risks and show our students that we still know how to laugh, to have fun, and to experience a little adventure in our lives. In doing so, we may encourage them to feel less conscious about themselves and to let go of their inhibitions and be free.

That same principle applies to parents as well—and grandparents, for that matter. My mother is approaching sixty (she's going to kill me), but when she plays with her eight-year-old grandson, she becomes a kid again. She rolls on the floor with water guns, plays SpongeBob video games, has pillow fights, and chases Austin from one end of the house to the other. They are like two peas in a pod, and he loves her so much. I hope that one day he realizes how lucky he is to have a grandmother who is so full of life and energy, and has such a wonderful sense of her youth.

I am certainly at an age where I am realizing how fortunate I was growing up to have her as a mother. She was always one second away from a laugh, a hug, or a kind word, and whenever I needed her, she was there. I can see her holding on to the end of my bicycle seat and running behind me, cheering me on and telling me I could ride on my own. I remember begging her not to let go, and when I turned around, I saw she was jumping up and down thirty feet behind me. I proceeded to crash in the ditch, but the point was that I had ridden that bike for the first time, and it was her spirit that made it possible. I remember trying to learn how to swim. I was in the deep end with my father, and he wanted me to just take off and try my best to make it to the other side. I was absolutely terrified, and I refused. Finally, my mother, who could not swim a stroke, stated that she would try it if I would. This came as a great shock to us all because Mom had declared that she would not be getting in that deep end. I can still see her trying to swim across. Bless her heart, she sank right to the bottom. Dad, Tassie, and I could see her on the bottom of the pool with her mouth wide open saying, "Help me!" Dad swam down as quick as lightning and got her, and to this day we still bring up that episode and laugh. Her mouth was *wide* open.

Something else happened that day. I also tried to swim across the deep end, and I made it. With Dad swimming beside me, Tassie standing with her hands on her hips, and Mom cheering from the shallow end, I made it. I love my mom for so many reasons, but one of the main ones is that she has never lost her sense of youth and her adventurous spirit. She has let down her guard and set an example for Tassie, Austin, and me that life is too short not to take a few risks and to live with a daring heart and a passionate spirit.

Finding Trust and Forming Bonds

I often hear from parents who say their child doesn't like them or they feel there is so much distance between them and their children that they don't even know them anymore. That usually seems to happen during the junior high years, and it seems to happen pretty much in every household.

The first thing I tell parents is that the children they knew and loved before adolescence will come back; it just takes a few years to get through that awkward stage. Love them, support them, and give them some space, and they will respect you for it in the long run.

The second piece of advice I give parents who don't feel a bond with their child is to go on some type of adventure. Whether it is rock climbing, rappelling, doing a ropes course, ice skating for the first time, playing paintball, running in a marathon, or going on rides at an amusement park, those types of activities tend to bond those who do them together.

There are many other options in addition to the ones I mentioned. Parents should pick whatever appeals to them and their child and go for it! I told that to a mother of two teenage sons in Montgomery, Alabama, and she asked me if I was going to pay her doctors' bills when she broke every bone in her body. I assured her that there are many different kinds of courses she could do with her sons where trained professionals will help to ensure their safety. She later sent an email to let me know that she had surprised her two sons by taking them to a local forty-foot climbing wall, and she and her sons made it to the top. She said she has never been so scared in her life, but she also said she will never forget her sons cheering her on as she made it to the top and that they actually didn't seem embarrassed to be seen with her. Sometimes when dealing with kids we have to take some risks, add some adventure to the relationship, and trust that it will form special memories and strong bonds in the long run.

Every time I go on a trip with my students, we become a much closer group that has much more respect for one another. After that time Derrick and I and the rest of the students rolled down those sand dunes, there was so much mutual admiration for one another that dealing with those students became effortless. When adults and kids experience some type of adventure, it pulls them together and creates a bond like nothing else. A few years back I went with my family to Disneyland. We went to ride the Log Flume, and as I was getting in line with my sister, her husband, and Austin, my nephew, I noticed that my mother was getting in line with us. I was shocked, but she said she felt she could handle the ride, so I didn't say anything. My mother riding the Log Flume. Oh, my goodness. I sat with my mom and told her that during the final drop we were going to raise our hands. She said, "Ron, you are crazy. I am holding on to this rail for dear life." But I said, "Mom, trust me. It will make it so much better." Just before the big drop I yelled to everyone, "Hands up!" As we went over the top, my mother and I locked hands and raised them in the air. When it was over, we just laughed and laughed and hugged. We purchased the photos of our "big drop," and I still have it sitting on my bookcase in my apartment. I love that picture because it reminds me of that special experience with my mom.

It's those types of experiences and moments that can

build a wonderful relationship between any adult and child. It builds trust, forms bonds, and provides memories that will last a lifetime.

Adventure Is Taking a Risk

Teaching in North Carolina had its share of challenges, but it was also comfortable. I was near my family and friends, and I knew pretty much everyone in the school and community. One day I saw a TV show about schools in Harlem that were failing. It showed overcrowded classrooms and students who were very bright, yet they had extremely low test scores. I can't really explain what I felt, but it was a mixture of desire to try to teach there and make a difference mixed with something that called within me to take a risk. I feel we need to challenge ourselves constantly, because when we become complacent or comfortable with our surroundings and situations, we don't seem to flourish or experience life in the same way. I made up my mind that I was going to push myself and take a risk: I was moving to New York City. My dad thought I was making the biggest mistake of my life, my mother was scared to death, my coteacher Barbara Jones told me I was crazy, and none of my students understood why I would leave them. It was the hardest thing I have ever had to do, but above all the other feelings there was a feeling of exhilaration, of passion, of adventure. I was more alive than I had felt in years.

At the end of the school year I packed my car and drove all the way to the big city. I didn't know anyone, and I drove around for hours trying to find a place to stay. I ended up at the YMCA in a room with no TV, no phone, no window, and no pillows or sheets; I wasn't aware I was supposed to provide my own. I first went to the Board of Education, and for those of you who have never experienced the New York City Board of Ed, it is like a huge airport crossed with a casino. There are long lines everywhere that lead to someone who may be able to help you or who may inform you that you're out of luck because you were in the wrong line all along. It is like taking a chance. I spent two entire days there, meandering around from line to line, until I was finally told that I should just put in my application and that I would be notified if a school wanted to hire me. I told the man I was speaking to that I wanted to teach in Harlem at a school with kids who really needed motivating, and he told me I would just have to wait until someone called me. He said if I tried to visit individual schools, no one would talk with me because that was not proper New York City procedure. I kept thinking, "Is this really a place that is trying to recruit new teachers?" It seemed as if they were trying to erect a barrier at every turn. I was so frustrated and wanted to just drive home. I remember I walked down four flights at the YMCA until I found a pay phone that worked, and I called my dad. He was sick and my mother was worried, and I almost said, "I'm coming home."

Then Dad said, "Well, I am worried, but I am proud of you, too, and I know everything's going to work out." God love him. I decided right then that I would ignore everything I had heard at the Board of Ed and that I would visit some schools in Harlem.

The next day I drove up and down the streets, past the famous Apollo Theatre and through the different areas of Spanish Harlem, until I passed a school on the right-hand side of the road. I had to park a ways down the street, and as I was walking back toward the school, I heard some sort of commotion on the other side of a door I was passing. I realized I was walking right past another school, but I never would have recognized it because it looked much like any other building in the city. I opened the door, and right in front of me there was a young man yelling at an older male assistant at the school. The boy claimed the assistant had tried to hit him, and the assistant was trying to restrain the sixth grade boy. They were both arguing, and the resource officer was saying she was going to call the boy's mother. My teacher reflexes stepped in, and I tried to pull the boy away from the assistant. Not knowing who I was, he surprisingly didn't resist and went with me. I followed the direction taken by the resource officer, and we ended up in the office. I sat the boy down in a chair and sat beside him. He was huffing and puffing, and tears were rolling down his face. He was breathing hard and taking huge breaths, and I didn't know what to do. Finally, I just leaned over to him and said,

"You know, I was breathing like that one time, and I passed out." "Huff . . . puff . . . huff . . . for real?"

We talked for about fifteen minutes, and I asked him questions like "Why are you so upset?" "If you could go back and change the situation, what would you have done differently?" "Do you like this school?" "What would you change about it?" After we had talked for a while, the boy said, "If there were teachers like you at this school, I wouldn't get in trouble so much, because you respect me and talk to me like you really care about me." I later discovered that there were actually some amazing teachers at the school who did care about the students and were doing a phenomenal job. On the other hand, I saw that the majority of teachers were dropping like flies. They would teach a week and then quit. Some stayed a month, others two months, but many of them did not make it through an entire year. Those kids had many abandonment issues, and after talking with that sixth grade boy, I knew that school was where I wanted to be.

I talked with the principal and told her I wanted a challenge. She told me that if I wanted a challenge, she was willing to give me one. She began to tell me about a group of students who were the worst she had seen in thirty years in terms of discipline and academics. I told her I was prepared, but I was really scared to death.

That year turned out to be quite a roller coaster for me; there were just as many hard times as good times. Moving to

New York City opened my eyes, my heart, and my mind to experiences I never would have had otherwise. I grew more as a person in that year than ever before, and it's all because I was willing to take the risk and follow my heart. At times it was definitely difficult, but I knew I was living. Every day was full of energy, excitement, and adventure, and I loved it. Looking back, I am so thankful I was willing to take that big scary step and just go for it. As teachers and parents we need to put that kind of fire, courage, and determination in the hearts of children. Help them face their fears, teach them when taking a chance is worth the risk, and give them the desire to follow their dreams.

Realistic Adventure

There are limits to what adults can and should do when adding adventure to a child's life. Each teacher has a different reality, personality, and expectations. In addition, there are always budgets, restraints, and other factors come into play. If it's in your nature to have an adventurous spirit, however, then express that and use it to motivate your students in whatever way you can.

Some teachers aren't up to conducting a large field trip, but there are some simple things that can be done to add some excitement and break up the monotony of the day-to-day routine. On beautiful weather days I would tell the kids to line up, and we would go outside and sit under a tree where I would teach. That takes little effort, but in the eyes of the students, it's heaven. It works best, however, when I am at a point where we are reviewing. It isn't good to try to teach something new or introduce a new subject while the students are outside. Some of my classes were not able to concentrate outside, so I would tell them that if they paid excellent attention for the first forty minutes of class, we could review outside for the last ten minutes. I was always surprised to see how those kids would sit up straight and on the edge of their seats at full attention. They wanted to go outside so badly that they would give me forty minutes of total dedication, and in my eyes the trade-off was well worth it.

Adventure in the classroom can be anything that brings the lesson to life. Some teachers bring in food from other countries, dress up as famous people in history, assign scavenger hunts where the students have to find information, or read a story so fervently that the students feel they are actually living the story themselves.

When I was in high school, I thought my civics class was extremely boring. It was just pages and pages of information about the government, and the teacher really didn't find a way to bring it to life. Then one day while we were learning about the judicial system, Ms. Cochran told us that we were going to conduct an actual court session in our classroom. Each person would have a role, and everyone would have to study hard and prepare for the activity. She explained that the lawyers would have to do the most work, and then she passed out folders that contained all our assignments. When I opened mine, I saw that I was to be the lawyer for the defense. When I walked out of class, Ms. Cochran said, "Ron, I gave you that responsibility because I know you will do an outstanding job." Hearing her say that meant a great deal to me, and I really started researching and digging for information. I did not want to let her down. I ended up actually going to talk with a real defense attorney to see how he would handle the case, and I got a lot of great ideas.

On the day of court I called up all kinds of witnesses, throwing them off track with difficult questions and accusations, and working every angle possible to show the jury that my client was innocent. It was exhilarating, and I loved it! That single day completely changed my attitude about that class. I tried a lot harder and wanted to impress Ms. Cochran. Just by adding that assignment and getting us all involved with what we were learning, she had sparked an interest in me that carried me through the remainder of the year.

Every year I try to add sparks to the curriculum just as Ms. Cochran did for me. One of my favorite activities involves the battle of the Alamo. After teaching the history of the event, I send home a letter to the parents and let them know we are going to re-create the battle at school using water balloons. They have to sign a slip giving their child permission to participate and agreeing to send their child with a white T-shirt and old clothes on a Friday.

The hardest part of this activity is that about 150 water balloons are needed. I ask a few parents to allow their children to come to school an hour early, and I set them up at the sink filling the balloons. Before they add the water, they place a few drops of red iodine in each balloon. When they are finished, they place them in huge trash cans at the back of the classroom.

At the end of the day I separate the students into their different roles. Some are Texans, such as William Travis or Jim Bowie, and some are Mexicans, such as General Santa Anna. They have all written a report on how it would feel to have been involved in the battle of the Alamo.

I place seven students behind a fence on the playground and tell them they are in the Alamo. I give them only 40 balloons to defend themselves. I then place the other students fifty feet away and tell them they are the Mexicans. I give each of them a red bandana to wear around their head, and they are given 110 balloons. If they are hit with a balloon by someone in the Alamo, they are out of the game and must sit down. Individuals in the Alamo, however, would not die if hit with a balloon because they are in the "fort." The battle is over when the Alamo is out of ammunition and someone from the Mexican army touches the fence.

The first year we did this activity, I didn't know how it would go, but as I stood back and watched the Texans work together and the Mexicans strategize on how to best attack the fort, it was impressive. The students were giving it all they had, and they were truly taking on the roles of the individuals they were acting out. I can still see the Texans as they were bombarded with all the balloons that Santa Anna's army had. All their T-shirts went from white to red, but they kept fighting. They wouldn't give up, even at the very end when their ammunition was almost gone and it was hopeless.

Those students still talk about that battle and many other events that we re-created. It brought what we were learning to life and made them feel a part of the history that normally was just confined to the pages of a book.

Adding an exciting activity, something different and something stimulating, to the classroom experience will help students have a better grasp of the material. They will become more interested in the learning process and for years to come will remember what has been taught. In order to truly reach all students, we must find a way to create that spark and motivate them to love learning.

✎ Being Smart with Adventure:
The Benefits of Organization and Preparation

Before teaching, I was never the most organized person in the world. In my high school yearbook there is a picture of my locker, and it is so full of papers and books that they are falling out on the floor. Once I started teaching, however, and I began to take students on trips, I realized how important it was to be organized and have my ducks in a row. The first field trip I took with students was to see a play that was just thirty minutes down the road, but getting all the paperwork done was like trying to saddle a wild mule. Everywhere I turned there were roadblocks. First there were no school buses available; next I found out I had turned in the request form late to the county, and the trip was denied. I had to get the principal to call to get it approved. Then I realized we would be missing lunch, so I had to arrange for us to eat at McDonald's, and I had to send home another letter asking the parents to provide money for their child. It was two days before the trip, and Mrs. Jones, my co-teacher, told me that was too-short notice to ask parents for money. I thought she was crazy, but sure enough I received two letters and one phone call asking why the parents weren't told the kids would need $5.00 before they sent in the permission form.

Drama. To top it all off, when we returned, I was greeted by the head cafeteria worker who informed me she would have appreciated knowing we were going on a field trip because she needed to take my students off the lunch count.

That was a small field trip. Imagine planning one to Washington, D.C., or beyond. It is a nightmare, and I don't think anyone realizes how hard teachers work to make those trips happen. I can remember begging my English teacher in high school to take us to London, and I remember wondering why her eyes would always bug out when she said no. I figured that we would just have some fund-raisers, that she could order the tickets and hotel rooms, and that then we would be good to go. My hat definitely goes off to all those teachers out there who take their kids on trips each year; whether they are overseas or in the States, it is a daunting task.

Some beginning teachers have told me that they wouldn't even know how to start planning a trip with their kids, and I tell them there are four main steps to making it happen.

A. Decide where you want to take the students and when you want to take them, and make sure you can tie in that year's educational requirements with the trip.

B. Get a good colleague and a parent to agree to help and to go on the trip. Make sure they are two respected individuals whom everyone trusts.

C. Write up a proposal for your students' parents that you will first present to the principal. This should be about six pages.

D. Get approval. After you have the proposal, you should take it to your principal. Sometimes I will talk with the principal before taking the time to do the proposal, but sometimes it is better to put the cart before the horse. When a person sees all the work you have gone through to prepare the proposal, it makes it harder for him or her to say no. If the trip is overnight or out of state, you will have to submit it to your Board of Education for approval. My county had a "no out-of-state trip" policy, but I showed up, gave them the proposal, and did a lot of talking about how the trip would help the students prepare for the end-of-grade tests. I have found recently that the best way to get approval for a trip or program is to mention how much it will raise the test scores. It works every time.

Once you have accomplished the four primary steps, you are ready to go. My main advice for someone attempting a trip with students is just to jump right in. Once you get the ball rolling, everything else will fall into place. If you look at the whole picture, it will be too overwhelming for you. Just plan the trip, get it approved, and take every other step as it comes. It isn't an easy experience, but when it is over, the results will be amazing and you can't imagine a more rewarding feeling.

Through Adventure We Discover a Lot About Ourselves

When we are placed in situations where we are challenged or pushed to our limits, we discover untested parts of ourselves and learn a great deal about what we are truly made of. I recently went rappelling off a cliff with a group of friends from college. We wanted to play survivor like the TV show, but in reality we love each other too much to vote any of us off, so we just camped in the wilderness for three days. While we were rappelling, my friend Erica did not want to do it. It was raining and the rocks were slippery, and when she looked over the edge of the cliff, she just flat-out refused. It is really a frightening experience, and I didn't blame her for being afraid. Nevertheless, we all kept encouraging her, and when I asked her why she didn't want to do it, she said it wasn't because of the rain or the height or the slippery rocks. She was nervous because she had gained weight and didn't know if she would have the strength to get herself down. I felt so bad for her because everyone else in the group was going to do it, and I didn't want her to feel left out. When I felt I had pushed her enough, I gave up. We all gave up. Then, right before we left, she said, "I'm doing it." She walked right over, put on her harness, and started making her way down the side of the cliff. Tears were running down her face, but she did it. She went slow and I could tell she was scared to death, but she made it all the way.

When it was over, I asked her what changed her mind, and she said, "I know I have gained weight, but in my life I have never used that as an excuse for not doing something. I have never let it stand in the way of any of my goals or things I wanted to achieve, and I wasn't going to start letting it have control over me today." To me, that was powerful. She learned so much about herself in that very moment, and now she tells me that whenever she considers doing something, whether it is at work or at home, she knows she can do it. She says, "I know if I went off that darn cliff, I can do anything." Experiencing adventure reveals strength within ourselves that we might never have realized was there.

Adventure Isn't Easy

My spirit of adventure is pretty large, and I try to share that with my students as often as possible. One dream I have had is to take a group of students to South Africa, and I doubted I would ever be able to make it happen. Since the summer of 2003, however, we have been gathering resources and making preparations, and I am happy to say that by the time this book is published, barring catastrophe, I will have made the trip to Johannesburg with twenty of my former students, ten from North Carolina and ten from Harlem. The students are now sophomores and seniors in high school, and planning this trip for them has been one of the greatest experiences of my life. It has also been one of the most daunting, challenging, problematic, and stressful experiences. I am losing hair at an alarming rate, and by the time this book is published, I will probably be in the major stages of the balding experience. I plan to put pictures of my kids and me on www.ronclark.info when we get back, so maybe you can check it out and see exactly how much hair I lost during the process.

When planning for an adventure, especially one that involves travel, unexpected things always pop up. It is necessary to realize that and prepare for it so that when it happens, you will handle it with the least amount of stress possible. I knew I would have to get passports for my students, but I didn't realize the complications that would arise. In order to get a passport, each child needed a certified copy of his or her birth certificate. Some of the students didn't have one, so we had to make arrangements to go to the courthouse to obtain new ones. Next problem: Some of the students were born in other counties and some in other states. Another problem: Even if I got the students to the proper courthouse to pick up a birth certificate, they had to have identification from the Department of Motor Vehicles to do so. Half of the kids didn't have IDs, so we had to go to the DMV to get them. Yet another problem: If you don't have a certified birth certificate, you can't get an ID at the DMV. It was a nightmare.

All I mentioned—along with getting passport-sized photos, filling out the paperwork, getting all the students to the post office to sign the correct documentation, and sending it off—was daunting, and that was just one facet of the planning for this trip.

One of the main reasons we are going to South Africa is so that we can visit schools in Soweto and deliver much-needed school supplies. I thought we would just have some fund-raisers and ship the stuff to Johannesburg, picking it up on our arrival. I didn't realize that every package we sent couldn't weigh more than sixty pounds and that each package would have customs taxes that needed to be paid by the receiver. It turned into a mammoth effort of getting the customs taxes paid and finding someone in South Africa to receive all the packages and keep them at a safe location until we arrived.

In addition, the kids had to get immunizations and we had to obtain health records for all of them. Plus there was the main effort, which was preparing the students for what they were going to see and experience on the trip. I am a firm believer that students going on a trip need to be completely prepared to understand everything they are going to see and experience. Addressing that for a trip to South Africa was an immense undertaking because the students' knowledge of the area was minimal, so I basically had to start from scratch. Some of the students had the impression that South Africa consisted only of jungles and tribes, and some were shocked to find out that a good portion of the population is Caucasian. We had to start from the beginning, with the history of the country, apartheid, the struggles the country has faced, and the issues it is dealing with today.

All in all, preparing for this adventure hasn't been an easy task, but without a doubt it is worth it. I know when I see my students walking through the streets of Soweto, delivering boxes of supplies and clothing to other students, that nothing can compare to their excitement and joy. Flying across an ocean, entering a new land, experiencing a different language, seeing a way of life so far removed from their own, touching lives, and making friends with a different culture—*that* is adventure. It is powerful and it is priceless, and it is definitely always worth the trouble. I am sure if you check out the picture on the Website, I may be bald but I will also be smiling from ear to ear and full of pride and joy.

Some teachers and parents have expressed to me that they would like to take more trips with their children but it is so expensive and time-consuming that it is really a struggle to make it happen. In response to that I simply say that if you wait until you have enough money to travel, then you never will. If you wait until you have enough time to fit it into your schedule, then that time will never come. Traveling and adding adventure to your life are things we must make sacrifices for. I wanted to take that trip to South Africa for years, but I was intimidated by what would be required to make it actually happen. Then I reminded myself of how we only have one chance at this life and how my biggest fear is that I will live with regrets. I didn't want to regret not taking this trip. So, without the proper resources, funding, information, or direction, I jumped in headfirst and got the ball rolling.

I can only hope that more teachers and parents will use that type of passion to create experiences for children. I am not saying I think all teachers should be hauling their classes to South Africa, but it is such a wonderful thing when teachers get their students out of the classroom environment and teach through travel and experiences. For those teachers I know it will be difficult to make it happen, but the rewards are great, and you will be giving your students memories that will last a lifetime. My mother still talks about how when she was in high school her class took a trip from North Carolina to New York City. She told me how my grandparents had to sacrifice a great deal to give her the money for the trip. Mom said when she found out about the trip at school, she knew she would be the only student who wouldn't get to go, but then Grandmother just told her, "We'll find a way."

When I was growing up, I used to love hearing Mom talk about how scared she was on the top of the Empire State Building, how excited she was when she bought Grandmother a discount skirt from Macy's, and how she still can't believe she paid $2.50 for a glass of orange juice. Those recollections have stayed strong in my mother's memory, and they are all thanks to a teacher at Washington High School who took a chance and was willing to get the ball rolling and make that special experience happen for those students.

✎ Adventure Builds Anticipation and
Fosters Improvements

When I sent the letters about South Africa to my students, I anxiously waited to hear from them and their parents. I answered the phone one night, and the person on the other end said, "For real?" I knew it was Val McCabe, and I knew what she was referring to. But I said, "Excuse me?" She said, "For real?" Again I said, "Excuse me?" "For real?" Finally I said, "Who would you like to speak to, miss," and Val said, "For real, Mr. Clark?" That was pretty much the response from all the students. I knew they would be excited, but I had no idea how shocked and thrilled these kids would be. After they found out about the trip, they were so excited. I asked them to do research, write papers, read books, and learn all types of information, and every single one of them did it without a moment's hesitation. Their work in school improved simply because I told them that I would be checking on their grades and that they needed to show me their appreciation by performing well in school.

I generally get similar reactions whenever I take my students on field trips. We always spend the weeks before learning about where we are going to visit. We learn the architecture of buildings, the history of the area, the backgrounds of the people we will be meeting, and other bits of information that help the students internalize the trip better. We did worksheets that taught them how to keep score before we went to bowl. We plotted our course on maps and estimated the amount of fuel we would need before leaving. We learned about sea creatures and erosion before heading to the beach. We basically do whatever it takes to prepare the students so that when they go on a field trip, they know what they are going to see and they are at a place where they are ready to learn and have an educational experience.

That process makes teaching very easy. Whenever I present new information, all I have to do is tell the students that what they are learning is needed for when they go on the big field trip. I say, "This is a field trip worksheet, so pay close attention and learn this information thoroughly." All the students get excited, mainly because the work has something to do with going on a trip.

Traveling excites us all. Experiencing something different, seeing a new place, and being in new surroundings is challenging and exhilarating. When you use that motivation to get kids to learn, not only do they retain information at a faster rate but they also want to learn because it is something they see as relevant, and something they will be using and experiencing in the near future.

3. CREATIVITY

The man who has no imagination has no wings.

—MUHAMMAD ALI

WHEN DEALING WITH CHILDREN, the greatest forms of creativity come out of necessity. We see a need to find a way to encourage kids to learn or to understand, and so we come up with as many ways as possible to pass on certain skills or knowledge. The best teachers and parents are the ones who are able to think outside the box and put themselves in the mind-set of the children they teach. They are able to find what works, and they are willing to try many different techniques until they discover the best solution to helping their children learn.

Creativity Excites and Inspires

Many kids' lives lack structure. Some spend their weekends with a different set of parents, some are never quite sure who is going to pick them up after school, some spend more time on the streets than they do in the home, and some have homes that don't even offer a stable environment. For all children, school should be a safe place. It must offer structure and stability, and teachers must make sure that there is a certain amount of organization and discipline in the daily routine. Once that is established, it is a good idea to throw some spontaneity into the day to keep the kids from getting bored. It's important for them to have a consistent schedule, but it shouldn't get to the point where it is mundane and every day is similar to the one before it.

One of my favorite books to read with fifth graders is *The Lion, the Witch and the Wardrobe,* not only because the kids enjoy it but also because it touches on issues of loyalty and honesty. In addition, it's a great book for kids because the author, C. S. Lewis, does a good job of maintaining the excitement throughout so that it never gets boring. I want my students to remember the story and how much they enjoyed reading it, so each year I try to do something extra to spice up and really bring it to life. We always read immediately after lunch, and one day we entered the room like normal and I began to recap what had happened in the book the day before. I waited patiently for one of the students to notice something unusual about the room, and suddenly one girl said, "Mr. Clark, I think something is wrong here." In the book four young children entered a closet and discovered it was a magical passageway to a land called Narnia where there lived an evil witch, the White Witch. I always joked with my class that perhaps the closet in the back of our room was the exact one from the story, because I had heard it was imported many years ago from England, where the story takes place. During lunchtime I had gone into the room, opened the closet, pulled out some coats, and thrown them on the floor. I then attached a long white piece of cloth to the handle, giving the appearance that it had been ripped off the White Witch as she entered our room.

As the students started to observe the scene, one by one they exclaimed, "Mr. Clark, I hate to say it, but I think the White Witch came through our closet." I thought for a moment and then with my most serious face said, "Well, if she came through our closet, then she must still be"— Hitchcock pause for dramatic effect—"somewhere in our school." I could just hear the 1940s horror movie music playing in their heads. One student said something about warning the others in the school, and I said that we shouldn't create a panic but should possibly look around the school to make sure nothing strange was going on. I told the students to stand back, and I jumped into the hall, fell to the floor, and rolled, à la James Bond, all the way into the bathroom. I could tell the kids wanted to burst out laughing, but they were keeping composure, playing the part. We stealthily walked down the hall, and when we got to the office, I asked Mrs. Bass, the secretary, if she had seen an extremely tall woman dressed in white walking down the hall. She delivered her rehearsed answer with perfection: "Why, yes, I did." I thought those students were going to fall out. Their eyes bugged as she said, "She went rushing by, and I yelled at her that she needed a hall pass, but she looked really pale so I figured she was running to the bathroom." I said thank you, and as we turned to walk away, Mrs. Bass added, "And, oh, she dropped this." She handed me a white scroll that was tied with a red ribbon. The kids were about to burst, but I was acting very calm as I accepted the note from Mrs. Bass, and they tried to follow suit.

We huddled in the hall, and I handed the scroll to Kenneth, telling the students I just couldn't bear to read it. Kenneth opened it and read the cryptic message:

> Through a closet full of clothes
> I make my evil way
> Into a school so full of fools
> They'll all regret this day
> For now I have
> The power to
> Steal all that makes them smart
> In the room most full of knowledge
> Is where I'll make my start.

The kids were all saying, "What does it mean?" and I will never forget the look on Marina's face when she said,

"The library!" We took off, and as we entered the room, there was Mrs. Sawyer, with perfect timing, standing with her hands on her hips over an empty cart. She was ranting that she thought the seventh graders had stolen her books. My most eloquent student, Brian, calmly placed his hand on her arm and said, "Mrs. Sawyer, I can tell you this much: It wasn't the seventh graders, but honestly, I don't think you can handle the truth." It was killing me not to burst out laughing. One book was left on the cart, and it took five minutes of standing there discussing and prodding before one student finally asked, "Why do you think she left that book?" Upon looking in it, they found another clue. Finally! We continued for the next thirty minutes, scouring the school for the White Witch and collecting other clues until finally we came upon the final note. It was attached to a basket of Turkish Delight. In the book, the White Witch put a spell on the Turkish Delight, and upon eating it a person would fall under her spell. The students all agreed it was best to destroy the candy, so we did, but not before Val McCabe sneaked a piece and put it into her mouth. Suddenly Val's eyes were rolling in the back of her head; she said she was dizzy, and she couldn't see! I told her to cut it out. It was time for math.

From that day, those students could not wait to finish reading the book. They knew the White Witch really didn't come through our closet, but they still felt they were a part of the book. That thirty minutes of make-believe had brought the story to life. Many of the students went on to read the other books in the C. S. Lewis series, and at the end of the year when I asked them to rank all the books we had read that year, *The Lion, the Witch, and the Wardrobe* was first on almost every list. To this day when I see those students, they still bring up the fun we had. It's possible to add creativity to any book you are reading or any subject you are teaching. Use techniques and whatever it takes to bring what you are teaching to life, to excite your students and inspire them to want to learn.

Using Creativity to Raise Test Scores

When I taught in North Carolina, it was always so difficult to raise reading scores, more so than with any other subject. I always immersed the students in all types of literature and genres; I read to them, read with them, and had them read silently. I modeled good reading strategies and taught them how to read with expression, to notice foreshadowing, and to detect context clues. I tried my best to get my students to love reading and to see how wonderful an experience it can be. You name it, I tried it, but nothing seemed to get the results I was looking for. I came up with an idea to go through some practice testing stories with my students to see exactly where the problem was. I allowed them to read the three stories themselves and answer the multiple-choice questions. That was a normal practice, but this time as we went through the stories together, I asked each child to let me know when he or she got to a part in the story that was confusing. I gave each child three small cards: a red one, a yellow one, and a green one. I asked them to hold up the red card if they were very confused, the yellow card if they were kind of confused, and the green card if they completely understood what they had read. After every sentence I had them raise their cards, showing me their level of understanding as they read the story to themselves, *not* as we were reading it together.

We did that procedure for all the stories and throughout all the questions. Almost every time the students showed a lack of understanding, whether it was with the passages or with the questions, it could be traced back to not understanding the vocabulary. Oftentimes they understood the story overall, but there were key words that threw them off and caused them to miss certain questions. I decided to take three new stories, and this time I introduced the vocabulary words to the students before we took the test. As we went through the passages together, I was pleased to see that almost everyone held up green cards every time I asked. I figured that in addition to all the other preparations with reading, I had to find a way to improve the vocabulary of my students. Just having ten new vocabulary words a week wasn't cutting it. I took out a set of practice tests they give us in North Carolina to use with our students, and I made a list of every key vocabulary word. I then did the same thing with the Standard Course of Study and other practice test materials we had at our school. I soon had a list of about five hundred words. I went through the novels we were going to read that year and listed all the key vocabulary. I wanted to read *A Wrinkle in Time* by Madeleine L'Engle with my students, but I knew the class I was teaching would struggle a bit, so I noted words from almost every page of the book. Soon I had a list of one thousand words.

I typed out each word and a short definition, and the result was a ten-page book, front and back, listing all the words. I got some 14-by-10-inch paper and made a cover that read, *Rockin' Words!* That next Monday I passed out the books to the students and explained why I was giving them the vocabulary packets and why those words were important. For the rest of the year we devoted a great deal of time to mastering the vocabulary. The first thing I did was teach them how to pronounce each word. We took it one page at a time. I would read one word, and the students would repeat it after me, making sure to follow along with their eyes. We then discussed the meaning of each word, and I asked the students to try their best to use the words in conversation and to point them out when we were reading together. I had each child bring in a set of index cards, and we made flash cards that had a word on one side and its definition on the other. We would get into pairs and practice, having one kid read the definition and the other try to name the word. We took tests, played games, wrote stories with the words, highlighted them in our stories, and had spelling bees.

I asked the P.E. teacher, Mr. Mitchell, to put the words in his lessons, and soon the kids were doing relays with the words where they would compete with another team. After each student ran his lap, he had to say the definition of a word Mr. Mitchell showed him before the next person could go. If he didn't know it, he had to run a half lap before the next person could go. When we went to the lunchroom, I would stand at the door and hold my set of index cards. I would show a word, and the student had to pronounce it correctly before entering. If a student got it wrong, I told him the correct way, and then he went to the back of the line.

Those kids were swarmed by those words. If we had a few extra minutes at the end of class, we would play this game called Elimination Ball that the students loved! With Elimination Ball, every child would stand up. I would sit in a chair that I had placed on top of my desk so that I was overlooking the entire class. I would then throw my soft globe ball to one student. Using my flash cards, I would say an antonym for a word, and the student holding the ball had five seconds to name the word I was looking for. If he got it wrong, he had to sit down and throw the ball to anyone of his choosing. I then asked the new person with the ball the same word. If he got it right, he got to pick one child to be eliminated from the game, usually someone he saw as tough competition. Kids usually saw this as a compliment, and so they weren't devastated to be out of the game. The person who is out sits down and throws the ball to a person of his or her choosing. The game goes on until one person is left standing, the grand champion!

This game works well and the kids love it, but I ran into a problem with kids not paying attention once they were out of the game. To solve that, I told them that if they were out of the game and someone dropped the ball, the first eliminated person to raise his or her hand was back in the game. The ball then went to that person, who was then asked a question.

This game can have many other variations depending on what fits you and your students. Instead of antonyms you can use definitions or synonyms, fill in the blank, or many other options. My class in Harlem even came up with a different variation called Super Elimination. We used three balls at once instead of one. I will never forget one day when my principal walked in during the middle of a game. There I was sitting eight feet in the air, and balls were going all over the place. She just opened the door, walked in, turned on her heel, and walked out. I tried not to let her bother me, because those kids loved that game.

I am sure some might say that the game wasn't really that educational and was wasting time, but because of that game there was a lot of studying and preparation going on at home. They wanted to be able to compete during the game. It got to a point where I made a chart that said Skill Level, and I listed all the students. If they won, they got three skill points; if they came in second, they got one point. If they were sitting down but got back into the game and won, they got four points. Those kids were bragging about their skill levels and checking that chart every day. They were into it, and I saw every kid holding those dictionaries and studying at lunch and recess.

The kids in both North Carolina and New York City were flooded with the words in their dictionaries, and it worked, because their test scores were through the roof. Every year after their end-of-grade tests the kids would want to tell me about all the words that were on the test that were also in our book. One year in North Carolina a question was "In the passage, what is the meaning of the word *agile*?" One of the choices was exactly the same as our definition. Teaching kids to love reading and to have all the necessary skills is important, but a key to helping students become successful readers and getting them to perform well on standardized reading tests lies in building their vocabulary. And it isn't "teaching to the test" because the vocabulary words are words the kids should know and need to know in order to become better readers.

On a side note, I ended up having my class read *A Wrinkle in Time* individually at home, and they loved it. After spending so much time learning those vocabulary words, reading that book was like instant gratification, because those words popped up in almost every sentence. Also, the program worked so well for my fifth graders that every grade at Snowden Elementary developed its own grade-appropriate dictionary. At the beginning of the year each student is given a one-hundred-word test, using words from their dictionary. There are five sections: multiple choice, antonyms, fill in the blank, matching, and form a sentence. Each test is graded by the counselor at our school and recorded. At the end of the year another test is given. The test for each grade is made up by a teacher from another grade. The counselor then grades those tests, and the scores are compared by individual student and also the class as a whole. It is a great indicator to see how far each class has come and to determine which teacher's techniques are the most successful when it comes to preparing the students.

There are now students who have had a *Rockin' Words* dictionary for the last seven years. There is no doubt that the concentration on vocabulary has helped the students become better readers and obtain much better scores on their end-of-grade reading tests.

Creativity Is Taking Advantage of "Teachable Moments"

At my first teachers' meeting in New York City, the principal outlined the schedule every teacher was supposed to use throughout the course of each day. For example, at 10:00 we would begin the math problem of the day, and at 10:12

we would begin the reading lesson. This was totally foreign to me because I was used to teaching one thing until the students understood it and then moving on, rather than having, essentially, a timer on my day. During the first week of school, the math problem of the day stated: "There are 435 members of the House of Representatives and 100 members of the Senate. If the total number of members of the House of Representatives remains at 435, how many states would need to be added to the United States in order for there to be more senators than representatives?" There are 335 more representatives, so there would need to be 336 additional senators. If there are 2 senators per state, then 168 states would need to be added to the United States.

As I started teaching that problem, I realized the students were completely confused because they didn't even know what the House of Representatives and Senate were. Not a single student got the question correct, and I know it wasn't because they couldn't do the math but because they didn't understand the content of the question. I took a piece of chalk and drew my best attempt at an outline of the United States on the board and started to talk about Congress and how representatives are chosen. The students seemed very interested, perhaps because it bothered them that they had absolutely no idea what the problem of the day was talking about.

Around 10:12 I heard a muffled cough at the door: "Hmph, hmph." I looked over to see the principal standing there. She said in a sweet voice that seemed to be attempting tolerance, "Mr. Clark, it's 10:12. Aren't we supposed to be on our reading lesson?" I was a bit taken aback, and I just said, "Yes, ma'am. But the kids didn't understand the problem of the day, so I am going over it with them." To my surprise she said, "But Mr. Clark, you just had the last twelve minutes to do that. Did you get started on the problem late?" I felt extremely uncomfortable, as if I was being undermined in front of my students. The worst thing in the world a principal can do is "talk down" or belittle a teacher in front of his or her students. I just replied, "No, we didn't start late. It's just a confusing problem and is going to take a bit longer." She grinned at me and then looked at the class and smiled at them in a way that seemed to say, "Bless your hearts. What slow learners you must be." As she walked out the door, I could tell she was fit to be tied.

Later that day I was called into her office, and I had to hear about how it is so important for us all to stay on the same page and that she felt I was insulting her in front of the students by not obeying her wishes to begin the reading lesson. I felt as if I was in the twilight zone.

Taking advantage of "teaching moments" is a quality that all great teachers share. When students show interest or when there is a spark or an eager question that is shared by all, there is no better time to veer off the course and use those teaching moments. When possible, it's always best to connect the new topic to the one you were covering. For example, as I went through explaining how we choose our senators and representatives, I was constantly referring to the numbers involved, going back to the problem and explaining how they should have used the new information to solve the question.

Whether you are a parent or a teacher, or both, this is a good philosophy to have: Don't be afraid to abandon a set plan or to scrap a lesson if an opportunity for learning presents itself that will be to the child's advantage.

Creative Discipline

My first year of teaching I had a very challenging class, and I was constantly trying to find ways to maintain order in the classroom. My co-teacher, Mrs. Jones, gave me an idea that I didn't think would work, but I tried it anyway. I had my students' desks arranged in groups of four, and I told the students that I would be monitoring which group was behaving the best and working well together. I showed them a trophy I had gotten out of the school awards case, and I said that I would place the trophy on the desks of the group that was the best behaved and staying on task. I would periodically move the trophy, depending on which group was working the best at the time. You should have seen the looks on those kids' faces; they wanted that trophy so bad, they couldn't stand it. That entire day was like a dream, with every group trying to outwork the others in order to get the coveted trophy. After school I told Mrs.

Jones, "This is brilliant! I will never have to worry about discipline again!" She just laughed and said, "Mr. Clark, you're gonna get about three good days out of that trophy, and then you can hang it up." She was right. The next day went well, and the third day was okay, but by the fourth day they really didn't care about the trophy anymore. Mrs. Jones told me that I used it too much too quickly. She said she would pull out the trophy only once in while, when she really needed to get the kids to focus. By having the opportunity to win the trophy only once in a while, it meant more to the students.

As a teacher, the more creative strategies you have in your bag of tricks, the better. Keeping discipline in the classroom is a constant struggle, and you have to be quick on your feet. Like the trophy technique, there are other tactics I used to get the kids to behave. All of them can be used only once in a while, however, or they will lose their effectiveness. I do a lot of work on building the class as a team, so sometimes I use strategies that will reward or punish the class as a whole. Occasionally I will place five circles on the board, and I will tell the class that every time someone misbehaves, I am going to color in one of the circles. If fewer than five circles are colored in before lunchtime, then the class will receive five minutes of extra recess. I also use it to lessen the homework assignment. If all five circles aren't colored, I will take off the assignment of the class's choosing. When I did my student teaching in college, and I taught eleventh grade history, I used the circles for homework with those students as well. The only difference is I used only three circles, because I had each class for only an hour. It worked just as well with eleventh graders as it did with fifth and sixth graders, but, again, it doesn't work if you use it every day. As a side note, if you are going to use a technique that holds an entire class responsible for the actions of individuals, it is best to offer rewards like more recess or less homework instead of punishing everyone with extra work that many in the class wouldn't deserve.

One technique I tried was effective, but it almost drove me crazy. I had seven boys in my class one year who could not sit still. They were constantly looking around, whispering, fidgeting with their books, and tapping their pencils, and all the while I was at the front of the class standing on my head, trying to make the lesson exciting. I came up with the idea to call the boys the "Magnificent Seven." I told them it was a club and that they were the only ones who could participate. I took a piece of typing paper, cut it in half, and drew a tic-tac-toe board on it. I then wrote Magnificent Seven at the top, and I laminated it. I made one for each of the boys and taped them on the top of their desks. I then went through Mrs. Jones's sticker box and got about five hundred stickers. The woman had enough stickers to cover a football field.

I told the boys that as I taught, if I noticed them paying attention and working well for an extended period of time,

I would give them a sticker and they could place it any-where on their chart. I told them that if they filled up an entire chart, they could trade it in and go to my supply box and select one item. Having a treasure chest in kindergarten works wonders, so I thought I would try it in fifth grade. Instead of toys, however, I had notebooks, pencils, some basketball cards, mini-staplers, and some other small items.

The plan worked really well. The boys were all trying to get those stickers, but I realized that they didn't really care about going to the supply box so much; they were just hav-ing fun competing against one another, and when they filled up a chart, they would keep it instead of turning it in. For two weeks the class was great, but soon the excitement of the stickers wore off for some of the boys. I eventually took away the charts from four of them because they were starting to cause problems, and it was obvious they didn't care any-more. Two of the remaining boys still cared somewhat, and if I needed to get them to pay attention, all I had to do was pull the sticker roll out of my pocket as I was teaching; they would sit at attention immediately, hoping they could earn a sticker. The final boy, Gray, made the whole experience worth it. He kept his chart on his desk for the entire year, and he went from being a holy terror in the classroom to actually paying attention, doing his work, and trying his best. Using the stickers doesn't work for every child, but for some it can do wonders. I realized after a few weeks that Gray was trying so hard not because he wanted the stickers, to compete with the other boys, or to get into the supply box. What he really wanted was attention and positive affirmation. Having me visit his desk periodically with those stickers was a constant pat on the back for him. He enjoyed that, and he needed it.

There are a lot of quick fixes that can be used for discipline, but the best technique I have found for long-term results involves getting the students to a point where they don't want to let you down. If the students respect the teacher and see that he or she cares about them and is truly trying to help them, they are going to be far less likely to cause problems in the classroom. There will still be discipline problems, but there will be far fewer of them, and solving them will be much easier. I have found that if students respect you and don't want to let you down, simply asking them to step in the hall and letting them know they have disappointed you will go a lot further than any other form of discipline that can be given.

Finding Creative Ways to Build Unity

One of the keys to having a successful classroom and a high-performing school is to create unity. When all the students feel ownership of their school and feel part of a place they are proud of, they are going to enjoy being there and become better students. I really enjoyed school-wide projects as a student and I also had a lot of fun with them as a teacher.

Oftentimes these activities would be in conjunction with fund-raising efforts for school improvements and other worthy projects. I know as parents it seems like every time you turn around the school has a new fund-raiser. It can be annoying and time-consuming, and I feel your pain. I cannot tell you the amount of Krispy Kreme doughnut syrup that has stained the backseats of my car and the money I have had to pay out myself because I bought wrapping paper from every student who asked me. It can definitely be a challenge for parents, but as a teacher I cannot say how much it meant when I had the assistance of parents who really worked hard to help us raise money. Schools are so often underfunded, and when we want to provide our students with something extra, our best option is just to raise the money ourselves. It is also great for the students to participate in some way because then they feel a greater ownership of the school and they see how their contributions make a difference. We used to have the oldest set of encyclopedias at our school. Most of them had torn edges and the B, K, R, S, and T-U were missing. Students who loved snakes soon learned to love lizards, and those who wanted to do a report on Martin Luther King, Jr., opted instead to choose George Washington Carver. We eventually had a raffle to purchase a new set, and the students sold more than four thousand tickets. Once the books were in place, those kids touched them as if they were made of gold, and we never had one turn up missing. They cared about those books because they had contributed to purchasing them for the school. Fund-raisers can do a lot toward building that type of feeling of unity.

At Snowden Elementary School we were in a low-wealth area, and we always had to find ways to raise extra money. Every year we would have Link Week, where each morning students could buy a link. Actually, we just took green and white construction paper, our school colors, and cut them into strips about an inch thick and three inches long. Each morning students were given the opportunity to buy a strip of the paper for ten cents. They would then add their strip to the end of the chain of links for their class.

Each teacher would start a chain of links that would hang from the ceiling and go all around the room. Every year it was quite a competition to see which class raised the most money and had the longest chain of links.

On the following Monday the links of every class would be taken to the gym and strung together, forming walls of green and white. We would have a big pep rally where they would announce the winning class. That afternoon the links would remain in the gym for the junior high's basketball games, and the money that we raised would go for various things, from school supplies to new uniforms to P.E. equipment. The great thing about it was that it didn't take much effort, all the kids were excited because they could all contribute and buy at least a few links, and it created a sense of unity and excitement. I have seen some schools use the links in a different way: Every class has a different color, and the links are placed from one end to the other of the hallway so that all the classes can see who is winning. Instead of having the students pay for the links, another option is to have links given to children every time they complete reading a book or have perfect attendance for an entire week. There are a number of ways to do it, but no matter which way is used, the links add color, excitement, and camaraderie to the school environment and are a great way to get kids motivated.

Another activity we did at my high school was a competition among the different grades. Each grade was given one big money jar that was sealed tight with electrical tape. The teacher in charge signed the tape and placed it in a certain way so that she would know if it was tampered with. There was a money slot in the top of the jar, and the object of the competition was for the students to collect as much money as possible over the course of a week. The problem was that only coins could be placed in the jar. If anyone placed paper money in the jar, that amount was subtracted from the total they collected. Throughout the week the grades had to carry the jar with them and keep a close hold on it so that no one from the other grades could get close enough to add any paper money to the jar. At the end of the week the class with the most money was named, and all the money collected went into a fund they could use for things such as prom decorations, field trips, or class T-shirts.

There are also ways to have school-wide projects that work to build unity without involving fund-raising. When

I was in high school, every year there was a door decorating contest, and each homeroom was responsible for decorating their homeroom teacher's door. We could make plans for the door during homeroom, but the ones who volunteered to do the artwork had to volunteer to stay after school to complete the project. Basically, we would just take a roll of construction paper and cover the door, cut out letters, and then come up with a design. There was always a theme, and we really had to be creative and make sure our door also had a message that went along with the decorations. It was such a great feeling to walk down the hall and see all the different ideas that people came up with and how much work they put into their designs.

The best principals put learning and the kids' enthusiasm ahead of all else, and they are willing to let down their guard, laugh at themselves, and take on whatever role is necessary to build school morale. At Snowden Elementary School in Aurora, our principal, Mrs. Roberson, was always willing to volunteer her services for any unusual methods we concocted to get the students motivated. I remember one time we decided to have a "Slime the Principal" contest. The students were challenged to read a certain number of books, and every child who met the requirements got to take a cupful of slime and throw it on the principal. I remember sitting in Mrs. Roberson's office and telling her of the idea. I was sure she was going to say I had lost my mind, but to my surprise she just said, "Mr. Clark, I'll do it for the kids." Mind you, when it came time for the sliming, Mrs. Roberson was covered from head to toe with every old piece of clothing she could find in her closet, and she wore the biggest sunglasses I have ever seen in my life. The kids loved it, and all of them, I mean all of them, read like crazy because they didn't want to be left out of the sliming.

The sliming project was excellent, but we had another plan just in case Mrs. Roberson wasn't willing to get slimed. It was called "Put the Principal on the School." With that project, each class that read enough books would get to go outside, sit on the grass, and look up at Mrs. Roberson as she sat on top of the school and read a storybook to the kids. Somehow Mrs. Roberson decided that being slimed was the better idea. I think having her get on top of the school building would have been fun as well, but it was far more exciting for those kids who got to throw the cups of slime.

I recently visited a community that has a wonderful program to encourage reading. It all started when the school challenged the students to read more than 10,000 books in one school year. Over time, the challenge grew to involve the teachers and everyone associated with the school, from the custodian to the superintendent. Eventually, the entire town set a goal of 500,000 books, and every individual who lived in the town was expected to read as much as possible in order to reach the total. When I visited, everywhere I went people were asking each other, "What book are you reading now?" "How many books have you read?" "Have you heard what the town total is so far?" Everyone was excited about it, and it gave everyone in that community something to talk about. It gave them a common goal, and it pulled them closer together. At the end of the year they had a celebration with bands, streamers, and the whole nine yards. It was a celebration for everyone, and the students from all the schools, their teachers, the administration, and nearly the whole town attended. That is a wonderful project that a local parents' group or PTA could start. You would need one person or a committee, depending on the size of the location, that all participants could report to whenever they had completed a book. Or there could be a Website that participants could go to and post the number of books they have read. I think students and adults as well would really enjoy going to the site each day to see how the number increases and gets closer to the desired total.

There are many other ways to be creative and pull a group or organization together. This year I attended the district-wide opening for Burnet Schools in Texas. I have been to many opening meetings, but this one was like nothing I have ever seen in my life. The event was held in a high school auditorium, and as the superintendent announced the names of the teachers and different schools, the entire high school band saluted with trumpets and revelry and excitement. There were banners and streamers everywhere, and the T-shirts of different schools represented school pride. On the stage were more than fifty gift baskets filled with all types of goodies that had been donated by local stores. The band played while names were drawn and different faculty ran up to get their prizes. Everyone was cheering and patting one another on the back, and the superintendent got up and said wonderful words of encouragement. Every individual who walked out of that building felt energetic and full of pride. Now that was a school opening.

However it is accomplished isn't important. What is important, however, is that teachers and school leaders find a way to be creative and put a spark in the school year that joins everyone together and provides a sense of unity and teamwork.

Using Creativity to Reach Your Audience

I was asked to speak to the student body of an at-risk school and it is an experience I will never forget. There I was, standing in front of five hundred uninterested teenage high school students, a skinny, pale, white man in a suit. It was obvious they weren't excited to hear what I had to say. It almost seemed as if it would have been uncool to act interested in my speech. As I began, I talked about passion, following dreams, setting goals, and being a leader. Man, I was really into it, arms swinging here and flailing there as I talked, but when it came down to it, I might as well have been talking to the wall. Students had started to whisper to each other, and I was about to lose the audience entirely. I decided it was time to reach into my bag of tricks. I signaled to the audiovisual man behind the stage to "hit it!" Soon music was pulsating throughout the audience. I jumped on the podium and broke into a rap. I had taken the words from a very popular song at the time and changed them to more appropriate lyrics. They went like this:

> You can find me in the class
> A bunch of good books with me
> I've got what you need
> If you need to learn to read
> I'm into good grades
> I'm not into dropping out,
> So come give me a shout
> If you know what I'm about!
> When I pull up out front
> See the bus on dubs
> When you read good books
> You can never get enough . . .

I threw in a few dance moves taught to me by my Harlem students, an Uptown Shake here and a Crip Walk there. Those kids were on their feet, shouting, cheering, and completely into it. For the remaining part of my speech they all sat wide-eyed and attentive, listening to every word I said. I will always remember what my college professor told me in speech class: "The most important thing anyone who stands before a group of people must do is know his audience." He was right. Whether you are teaching your class, talking to your own kids, or giving a speech, it is crucial that you know the personality of the group you are speaking to and that you find a way to relate to them and get them to the point where they are willing to listen.

As a parent or teacher it's also important that we remember not to take ourselves too seriously at times. We may have to laugh, dance, sing, make funny faces, or do the unusual, but we have to be willing to let down our guard and have fun with education. Sometimes it takes creativity, something different, something dramatic to catch the attention of students, to earn their admiration, and to get them to respect what you have to say.

Creativity Leads to Respect

When people see that you are putting a lot of effort into helping them, they will always show greater respect for you. Going out of your way and being creative will not only impress people but will be greatly appreciated. I remember one Christmas when for the Secret Santa drawing I pulled the name of a teacher who was never especially friendly to anyone else. I tried everything I could to make the gift I put in her box every day something special and creative. For the final day I had written a long poem about how great a teacher she was, and I had it framed, with pictures of her and her students going around the sides. I could tell it meant a lot to her, and every day after that she was nice and friendly toward me. She could tell I went out of my way to do something nice for her.

My father and I didn't have the closest of relationships when I was growing up, but he was an excellent parent and I respected him a great deal. During my third year of teaching, my students were always saying they wanted to meet him and my mother. I had told so many stories about them, that I think they wanted to see if they were all true. My parents agreed to visit the class, and when they walked in, I was shocked to see them carrying all types of materials. My mother had baked her mouthwatering sea foam candy, her own secret recipe, and all the students loved it. My father had created a huge three-sided display filled with pictures of the construction he was doing on a new hospital. He told the kids about his job and showed them the pictures. I was so impressed at the time and effort he had put into the presentation, but then my mouth dropped to the floor as he turned the display around to show the other side: It was full of pictures of me from when I was a baby all the way to the present day. My students went crazy, and I didn't think my parents would ever stop laughing. I got to go through each picture and explain what each one meant, and my parents were there to verify that all the stories were true. I could tell as I looked through the pictures that my father had spent a great deal of time working on the display. He was very busy with his job, and for him to take the time to do something so creative and thoughtful meant the world to me.

After that, I started looking at my father differently, and our relationship started to change. Perhaps I was just growing up and starting to mature, but whatever caused it, I started to see how much he cared about me and how wonderful he was to go out of his way for me time and time again.

Teachers are invested in students but are never as emotionally involved as the parents. Remembering to take the time to do special things for our children and show them how much they mean to us can never be done too much.

4. REFLECTION

By three methods we may learn wisdom:
First, by reflection, which is noblest; second,
by imitation, which is easiest; and third,
by experience, which is bitterest.

—CONFUCIUS (C. 551–479 B.C.)

For years children have marked their height on the kitchen wall to track their growth. It's important, however, for children to be able to see how they have grown and improved in all areas, not just their height. Learning from our mistakes and holding on to our memories help us become deeper individuals with a better sense of who we are and how we choose to live our lives.

Providing Memories of Children's Successes and Accomplishments

At the end of every school year I always have an awards ceremony for my students. I expect a great deal from them throughout the year, and when that last day of school arrives, I don't want my class to walk out the door with just a "great job!" I want to create something special, a celebration that acknowledges all the hard work, rewards the excellence of each student, and provides closure for the year.

The way I organize this event can be quite pricey. I usually have tablecloths, doughnuts, juice, balloon bouquets, and numerous medals, plaques, and trophies. In North Carolina we usually had the ceremony at picnic tables on the water. In New York we had the event in the cafeteria. Where it is doesn't matter. What does matter is that parents, friends, and family are invited and that there are plenty of awards to go around marking the success of the year.

I usually do fund-raising to cover the cost of the event, but one year in New York the final week was upon me before I knew it, and I hadn't had time to get any funds. I had ordered the awards about two weeks earlier, but I just hadn't gotten around to obtaining the money for them. I had about five messages on my phone from the trophy store, and I had to do something. I was talking with Alice, a straight-talking, no-nonsense, born-and-bred New Yorker with two-inch bright red fingernails who was an assistant at the school. I told her about my money problems, and she asked me in her thick accent if I had been given my June check. We had all been given our checks early because it was the last week of school, but the banks wouldn't cash them until the following week. She then said, "All right, I got you. Meet me after school. I have someone who will cash that check."

I was a bit skeptical, but after school we met in the office, and Alice led me out of the school and down past 125th Street in Harlem. We walked and we walked, and every time I asked where we were going, Alice would just say, "I got you," so soon I just gave up and kept following. We finally turned down a street and into a small alleyway. I noticed a line of about thirty people coming out of a door that looked as if it led into some kind of office. It seemed strange to have an office there in the middle of an alley, but I didn't say anything. Alice and I got in line, and I was like "Alice, where in the world have you brought me?" I was getting a lot of stares in my blue suit and Scooby-Doo tie, and I was not in the least bit comfortable. Alice replied, "You want to get them trophies for those kids or not?" I couldn't argue there, so I just remained in line, trying to hunch over as much as possible and focus my eyes on my shoes. We finally reached the doorway, and I saw an even longer line inside. To the right was a man standing behind a counter. Alice whispered to me, "There is a shotgun under that counter, so don't make any sudden movements, all right?" I just gulped and looked toward the head of the line. There I saw a desk with stacks and stacks of money all over it. On each side of the desk were huge men with their arms crossed. Behind the desk sat a balding man of about three hundred pounds. His white shirt was unbuttoned about four buttons to reveal multiple gold chains resting on his bushy chest hair. Alice whispered, "He's the boss. No sudden movements, and for God's sake don't open your mouth. Just hand him the check and take whatever he gives you back."

When we got to the desk, I could feel all eyes on me. I was so nervous that the sweat from my hands had smudged areas of the check, and my handprint was nearly visible from where I had been clutching it in my hand. I just handed him the check and waited. He looked at me and then at the check, then me and then the check. Finally he said, "What do you want?" I wasn't expecting a question. I looked at Alice, and her eyes were bigger than her hoop earrings. I looked at the boss, and in my undeniable southern drawl I said, "I want some money for that check, please, sir." I could feel Alice turn away from me, and the boss looked at me as if I was a fool. He said, "I know that, Opie, but how much you want to get for this check?" Out of nervousness I just said, "I guess whatever you'll give me." He tapped three times on the table with his finger, and the man to his left counted out some money in twenties. He handed it to me without as much as a word. Alice and I turned and left. He had given me 80 percent of the check. He had kept my food for the month, and I was not happy about it. I was glad, however, to be alive and thrilled that the ceremony would go on.

On the last day of school the students arrived dressed

in their best Sunday clothes, along with their parents and family members. They sat at brightly decorated tables in a room filled with balloons and streamers. I stood at the head table, which was full of various awards and trophies of different sizes. Each award was engraved with the child's name and with the reason for recognition. These were really nice trophies. I could have just made certificates, but I needed it to be special. I needed those kids to feel special and to feel that their achievements were worthy of only the best.

Parents and students followed along on the program as I read each award. I talked for a minute about the student's success that year, without revealing his or her name. I built up the anticipation, and then I said something to this effect: "And I am so honored and proud to announce that the award for the most improvement in reading goes to a remarkable student with so much potential . . . DeQuan Johnson." Everyone applauded, and DeQuan beamed as he came up, shook my hand, and received his award.

Each year when I do that ceremony, the students always hold themselves high, I get all choked up, and several parents cry. One man in Harlem cried so hard that I had to raise my voice to talk over him. He didn't speak English, and after the ceremony his daughter told me, "He is crying because when he moved our family to America, he did not know if his children would be successful in school. Today he has realized he made the right decision."

Moments like that make going to visit a mafia boss to illegally cash a check seem sensible.

I am not saying that teachers should turn to a life of crime or spend their own money to make events like that happen. In fact, it is a shame how much money teachers are already spending. Each year classroom teachers in the United States spend over one billion dollars of their own money on school supplies. What I am saying, however, is that money is out there. Sometimes all it takes is making a few calls to local businesses and explaining why you need funds and how it can help children. If that doesn't work, a good doughnut sale can net a few hundred dollars, and that's more than enough for a wonderful awards ceremony. However it is accomplished, we need to do whatever it takes to give students moments where we lift them up, make them feel rewarded, and give them a sense of pride in all they have accomplished.

Reflecting and Finding Ways to Improve

One of the best qualities of an exceptional teacher is that he or she learns something from every lesson that is taught. There is always room for improvement, and I used to feel sorry for my first period history class because by the time sixth period rolled around, the lesson had become so much more polished, organized, and exciting.

I remember one time when I was required to put

together a portfolio, and I saw where they wanted me to critique a video of myself teaching. I thought that was the craziest thing I had ever heard. I mean, geez, I was already there for the lesson one time. I knew what I said and how I taught. I did as I was instructed, however, and when I watched the video, I was in shock. There were times when I felt I had talked too fast and others where the students probably could have used more explanation, but I just went on with the lesson. I noticed that I was standing more toward the left-hand side of the room, and I didn't call on Terry the entire time even though he raised his hand for every question. There were a lot of things the video revealed to me that I never would have realized otherwise. It is a very humbling experience to watch yourself and see your flaws on tape, but it is also a wonderful learning experience that can only lead to better teaching in the future.

My co-teacher, Mrs. Jones, has put together binders over the years that contain all of her math lessons. She keeps these binders at the front of her room, and each day she can just turn to the next page where she will find overheads, worksheets, lesson plans, and notes. In the notes she has made suggestions for how to make the lesson better. Every year her teaching becomes more organized and more efficient because she always takes the time to add key points to her lessons when she notices ways to improve them. She is truly a master teacher, and I know a great part of that is due to her experience and her dedication to taking note of how she teaches and what works and what doesn't.

✏ Reflection in Writing

Whenever I think about my years in elementary school, many memories are just as clear as if they happened yesterday. I remember a teacher making me copy the entire S section in the dictionary because I talked so much. I remember when Mrs. Woolard fainted in third grade while she was checking Pam Beavers's head for lice. We all thought for sure Pam was infested, but actually Mrs. Woolard was pregnant. I can still see Stephen Paszt throwing up on me in fifth grade, and Mrs. Edwards giving me one piece of caramel candy to make me feel better. One piece of candy? That boy ruined my coat!

Of all the years and memories, however, my sixth grade year is clearer than any other time. I can even remember the order Mrs. Walker taught the subjects, the bulletin boards on the walls, where I sat in relation to my friends, and my feelings as I went through that entire year. The reason is that Mrs. Walker had us keep a diary, and each day we had to write "emotions," how we felt and what was going through our minds. Our diaries never left the classroom, and on that final day of school when Mrs. Walker told us we could take them home, I walked out of that class feeling as though I was holding a million bucks. I can never thank her enough for giving us five minutes each and every day to write. In between my writings about my desire for a new pair of parachute pants and how I wanted to outrace Hallet Moore, I shared many things about projects we did that year, the things I learned, and what excited me most about school. In addition, there was page after page where I expressed feelings about myself, my dreams, and my goals in life. I still have my journal to this day, and it will always be one of my most cherished items.

I believe every parent and teacher should encourage children to write down their feelings daily. Not only is it a way to sort out your feelings and emotions, but it is also a way to preserve memories that otherwise would fade with time. My only regret is that I did it for only one year. I wish I had had more teachers like Mrs. Walker who made the time and persistently got me to record a special part of my life.

Reflection Through Memorization: Listen, My Children, and You Shall Hear . . .

When I was in fifth grade, Mrs. Edwards had us memorize the prose poem "Paul Revere's Ride" by Henry Wadsworth Longfellow. If we said twenty lines, we got one piece of caramel. I swear that woman held on to those caramels as if they were priceless. If you said thirty lines, you got two pieces of caramel, and so forth. At the time I didn't understand why it was important, but when I look back, I can

hope by doing so that they will have a stronger connection to the lesson that I was teaching and that they will have concrete information they can take with them. Just as Mrs. Edwards did, I always have my students memorize "Paul Revere's Ride." In addition, we also memorize math songs, the states and capitals, famous scientists and their accomplishments, the presidents, famous speeches by Abraham Lincoln and Martin Luther King, Jr., explorers, famous dates, monuments around the world, and a number of other bits of information to go along with whatever we are learning. It is a simple addition to the curriculum, and I just ask the students to work on it at home. No classroom time is spent on the assignments other than times when I have each student stand up and recite the necessary information.

One thing I always make sure my students learn is the national anthem. It bothers me so much when I see people on TV mumbling the words, standing with their hands in their pockets, or talking to each other when they should be paying tribute. Usually, athletes aren't the best role models for standing at attention during the anthem, but something happened recently that really impressed me. I was at an Atlanta Hawks game, and they were playing the Cleveland Cavaliers. During the singing of the national anthem I saw a group of teenagers in the front row taunting a famous Cavalier player, Lebron James. They kept yelling at him and pointing at the caps on their heads that named another basketball player. They just kept taunting Lebron during the anthem, but even though they were only about ten feet from him, he acted as if he didn't hear them and he continued to stare at the flag. I was so angry at those kids that I didn't know what to do. I wanted to say something to them myself, but then during the middle of the song, Lebron finally acknowledged them. He turned and said in a deep and adamant voice, "Have some respect and put those hats over your hearts." He then turned and went back to silently staring at the flag. Surprisingly, the teenagers took off their hats and did as they were told. For a player of eighteen years of age, I thought Lebron's comment showed a great deal of maturity, and I gained respect for him. So many kids, however, like those teenagers who were yelling, don't show respect during the anthem, and so, with my kids, we practice over and over not only the words but also how to stand, how to act, and why it is important to show respect for our nation.

In terms of having students memorize and recite information or give speeches, some students and many adults are simply terrified of standing in front of a group of people. Actually, that is one reason that I have them do it in fifth grade. I know the older they get, the more frightening it will become. If they get used to it and develop a way to cope with it then, they will have an easier time as they get older. I have had some students, however, who were so scared that I was afraid it was bothering them too much. In those cases I tell the students that they can stand and recite the information together in a group of three, but I warn them that their grade will be the same for everyone in the group, so they had better make sure they are all prepared. If one person messes up, it will affect everyone's score. That actually works out well, because the kids tend to study harder and work well as a team.

I would encourage every parent and teacher to incorporate some memorization into their lessons. It doesn't have to be often, but doing it once in a while will help your students have a better connection to the material you are presenting and give them a great sense of accomplishment.

I will offer a final word of warning to any parent or teacher expecting children to memorize information: Be prepared to learn the material yourself, because the first question you are going to hear is "Have you memorized this yourself?"

Reflecting on a School Year

As I get older, I am starting to appreciate my parents a great deal. I call them daily just to talk, to see how they are doing, and to find out about their day. They are so hilarious and always up to something, and every day there is some new story to be told. Early last year I told my mom that I don't know what I will do when the day comes that I might not be able to pick up the phone and hear their voices and experience life with them. That thought scares me.

On Christmas morning we always save the "special" presents for last. My final gift came from my parents, and as I opened the beautiful blue and silver box, I saw a scrapbook. I turned to the first page and saw a letter to me from my mother. It explained how each day throughout the entire year she had recorded Dad's and her life, creating a journal of letters that included her thoughts, funny stories, pictures my father had taken, mementos, advice, and memories. She said that one day they won't be with me but that they wanted me to be able to pick up that book and feel as close to them as possible.

I love my parents so much for taking the time to create such a special gift for me. Creating a book of memories allows us to almost travel back in time, touch yesterday's memories, and relive the past.

For many schools, especially high schools, it's normal to have a yearbook, but it's not common for a class to have its own book of memories. This is usually because of a lack of funds or the time required to put together such a collection of pictures and notes about the year. It can be done, however, and when completed, it will be well worth the effort.

When I taught in North Carolina, I conducted a year-long project with my class, and we put so much time and energy into it that I wanted to find a way to preserve all that the students had learned. I contacted the company Lifetouch and found out that for about $1,000 our class could produce our own softback yearbook. The cost included all of our film and developing along with the production kit.

Lifetouch would provide us a total of sixty copies of the completed book. The class conducted three Krispy Kreme doughnut sales, and we had the money in no time.

Throughout the year the students stayed after school to place pictures and their memories of the year onto the pages Lifetouch provided. There were times when the students made grammatical errors, and there were times when they didn't choose the best picture or went outside the page lines; nevertheless, I made as few comments as possible because I wanted the book to be their own. When all our pages were complete, we sent in our packet to Lifetouch and anxiously awaited our completed books. On the day they arrived, I felt like a little kid as I placed the big box in front of the class and we tore through the wrapping. When I pulled out the first copy, there were ooohs and ahhhs throughout the class.

One of the most wonderful parts of the project and the book involved a boy named Marus. He was a very quiet child, and teachers in the past had mislabeled him by saying he was learning disabled. He often kept his head down, and his work was not on grade level, but there was something about Marus and it just took a while to see it. When we discussed in class the options for the cover for our book, the students decided it would be neat if they drew the cover themselves. Our project involved places all over the world, and the students began to draw all different ones, from the White House to the pyramids of Egypt to the Great Wall of China. The students used all kinds of crayons, markers, rulers, pictures, books, and anything they could get their hands on. Marus, however, sat by himself, using nothing more than a pen and the edge of a sheet of paper to form lines on his drawing. As I stood over him, he crouched over his work so that I couldn't see it. I could tell he was holding his breath and very nervous. I quietly said, "Let me see, Marus." When he pulled himself up, I saw the beginnings of what turned out to be the most amazing book cover in the world. What you see here was done completely by Marus without the use of any pictures or even a ruler. These images were locked in his mind, and as he used paper edges and his favorite pen to develop his masterpiece, the look on his face was one of determination, wonder, and pride.

Soon after, I had Marus tested, and we found out that Marus is actually a gifted child but is only able to express his gift through art.

Discovering Marus's talents was only one of the wonderful benefits of doing the yearbook. My students learned a great deal about design, structure, organization, editing, and conveying their emotions in writing. They wrote a book from beginning to end, and their pride in that accomplishment was written all over their faces. A school year is such a wonderful period, full of excitement, memories, knowledge, and growth, and for those students to have all those experiences combined into a book that they would be able to keep forever and share with their children and grandchildren was an amazing thing. I am sure many people reading this would

love to have a book of memories from their fifth grade year. Most of us probably have no idea of all the things we have forgotten.

Imagine getting to look through that book and seeing your thoughts as a ten-year-old, remembering all the faces of your classmates and dear friends, and seeing all the accomplishments of that year and all you learned. For any teacher to create such a special gift for a class is, I feel, well worth the time, energy, and effort.

During my first year in New York City, I was too busy to worry about doing a yearbook. I was too busy getting my feet wet. In cases like that, taking on such a task isn't a good idea. The second year I really wanted to do a book with my students. There were, however, thirty-seven kids in the class all day, and all of my time before and after school was spent tutoring and with detention. I just couldn't find the time to begin the book. What I did was take pictures as often as possible, and I asked my students to write comments about every trip, project, and experiment we had in the class. I kept all that information in a folder. One week before the end of school, I pulled out all the pictures and comments, and I started to glue-stick them in various collages. (To whoever invented the glue stick, you rock!) I also sent a letter home to the parents and asked for a baby picture of their child. I said it was for a class project. I then had my students fill out a form that included such things as favorite food, best memory from this year, what will I be doing in ten years, and other such categories. For an entire weekend I stayed busy formulating a book for the kids. On the front page I had a wonderful picture of all the students out on the playground, with the words "The Amazing Class 6-211" at the top. On the following pages I had each child's class picture along with his or her baby picture, and to the right of the photos I had all the information that child had filled out on the form. The rest of the book contained pictures of our trips, things we had learned, the science fair, the sixth grade graduation, and other memories of the year, along with different quotes I had gathered from the students.

Once that was complete, I went to a local office supply store and purchased forty binders. Each page had a clear cover so that once I placed in each sheet, it would not bend or tear or collect stains. I purchased two color ink cartridges, and that Monday after school I ran off all the copies of the book. The amazing Mrs. Scofield, the science teacher, then helped me stuff the sheets into each of the binders. On the last day of school we were in the auditorium for an assembly. I told the students that I had a graduation present for them and that when they went into the room it would be on their desks. When the students walked in, they all looked suspiciously at the book. They sat down and one by one opened the pages. I expected them to scream and shout, but you could have heard a pin drop. They just sat quietly, looking closely at each page, drinking it in before turning to the next. It was a wonderful moment. I have never seen students show appreciation more sincerely than they did that day.

A teacher's job is never done, and with test scores, teacher meetings, paperwork, lunch duty, paperwork, parent conferences, paperwork, and lesson plans, there never seems to be any time to actually teach. With all of that, it seems improbable to have time to create a memory book for a class, whether going through a yearbook company or constructing it yourself. If time can be found, however, you will be creating a special gift that will be cherished for years to come.

Reflecting on Growth

Whenever possible it is highly successful when we are able to show children exactly how much they have learned and have grown over a school year. On the first day of school I always give my students a blank map of the world. I ask them to fill in as many continents, countries, states, capitals, mountains, and bodies of water as they can. Some fifth graders will tell me they don't know any places. I promise them that I won't look at their maps and for them to just try their best. When they are finished, I gather the papers, keeping my eyes toward the ceiling, and then I stand on my desk and place the papers on the highest shelf in the room, promising to leave them there.

Throughout the year I really stress geography and the cultures of civilizations all over the world. I want my students to have a better understanding of other nations, religions, beliefs, and ways of life. I think it is a shame how little many kids seem to know of other cultures and people. I can remember that when I was in school, teachers always seemed to focus on the United States, but we learned very little about other countries. Some students, however, aren't even provided with a good understanding of the United States.

One of my favorite questions to ask children, not only my students but any child, is "What country do you live in?" They will almost always say their city or state. When I visited Japan, I went from class to class, and was introduced to the students and said a few words. The students always asked where I was from, and I would say, "The United States," and they would laugh. They would then ask, "Where in the United States?" and I would say, "North Carolina." Many would then ask, "Oh? Do you live in Raleigh or Charlotte?" It amazed me how much they knew of the geography of our country. These kids were ten years old, and yet when I ask students here to name our country, many cannot do so.

That is why I spend so much time stressing geography in my classes. In North Carolina I had a wonderful wall map, and whenever we read about a new location or the name of a distant land appeared in our reading, I would fly over to the map and point out the place and where it was in relation to us. We had map tests where the students had to learn not only the locations of countries but their languages, currencies, capitals, religions, and customs. We played games where everyone would stand up and I would point to a location on the map and ask the first person to name it. If that person got it right, he or she stayed up; if that person got it wrong, he or she sat down. It was a fast-paced game, and the students had only three seconds to name the locations. The kids loved, loved, loved that game, and soon all the students could name any state, country, mountain range, and body of water I selected.

Actually, teaching all that information wasn't in the curriculum, and when I got to New York City, I had some problems. First, there were no wall maps in the room, so I had to use overhead maps whenever I wanted to point out a location. Even that was challenging because there was only one working overhead in the school that all teachers had to share. Second, the administration didn't understand why I was spending so much time teaching something that wouldn't even be on the end-of-grade tests. That was a definite roadblock for me, and I had to make sure I had all my other bases covered first and that my students were all fulfilling the standards and requirements of the State of New York. To help battle that problem, I selected several novels that dealt with countries around the world, and in social studies I didn't only teach the history of the United States but I also taught how the United States relates to other places and locations. In science we studied the currents of oceans around the world, and when I discussed evaporation and precipitation, I labeled the bodies of water with the names of lakes around the world. When I divided the class into seven teams in physical education, I gave each team the name of one of the seven continents. When I taught health, I put up charts to show countries around the world and their health rates, such as their life expectancies and the infant mortality rates. When we celebrated holidays, I put up a map to show what countries around the world also celebrated our same holidays. In short, I used every opportunity I had to incorporate geography into our class.

On the final day of school, one of the last things I always do is pass out a blank map of the world. I ask the students to fill in all they know. It usually takes about an hour. The students are writing as fast as they can, labeling mountain ranges, detailing capitals and other major cities, writing their languages and customs out on the side. It is wonderful. I then stand on my desk, retrieve the first tests, and pass them back. Total shock. The students cannot believe the difference and the progress they made over the course of the year, and they are simply shocked. Most students will label well over 200 locations. To go from that map that is basically empty to one that is completely labeled and shows a wealth of knowledge is gratifying for everyone.

No matter what the subject, showing kids how much they have learned and how far they have come is a great way to build confidence and give them a sense of accomplishment, and the process can actually be an easy one. You can compare writing samples, math tests, and any number of assessments that will show students how much they have learned.

Parents can also take part in this process. One of my dreams is that every home in America would have a world map on the refrigerator. Whenever a location is mentioned on the TV, in a movie, on the news, or wherever, take the time to point out on the map where the place is located. Go to my Website, www.ronclark.info, and under Teacher Resources click on Printable World Map. Print it out and use it to test your children and help them practice. Do your best to explain to your children about other places around the world, because in some classrooms a complete view of the world isn't being presented.

Sharing Our Experiences with Others

One of the main reasons so many of us take pictures isn't only because we want to see ourselves but because we want to share them with others. Whether we have a journal, a yearbook, a photo album, or other mementos, it gives us a wonderful way to share our experiences with our friends and family, and help them understand us better.

My co-teacher in North Carolina, Barbara Jones, does a wonderful activity with her students every year. On the last day of school she has them write a letter and address it to "Dear New Sixth Grader." In the letter they are to tell all about what they learned that year, noting their best memories and why they loved sixth grade. They are then supposed to give advice to the new students and tell them how to be successful in Mrs. Jones's class. She then collects the letters, and on the first day of school in the fall, she gives out one letter to each of her new students. It is always a special moment for those young kids to receive words of wisdom and advice from the new seventh graders.

✐ Reflection Allows Us to Hold On to Memories Longer

I am very thankful that I have complete memories of sixth grade. Thanks to the journal I kept that year, I will always have vivid thoughts of the surprise party we threw for Mrs. Walker, the crush I had on Lisa Tepper (even though it was a love/hate relationship), the anticipation of the art contest, racing Hallet Moore each morning, and hoping each day that I would walk into the lunchroom to the smell of the best vegetable soup in Beaufort County. I hope that years from now my former students will also look at their yearbooks and journals and smile as fond memories come back to them as well. I know that the special book my mother made for me will touch me as I read it over and over again no matter how much time passes, and I can never thank her enough for giving me a gift that will allow me to hold on to my special memories of her and my father.

It does take effort and it does take time, but helping someone record memories and reflect upon the past is a very special gift.

5. BALANCE

There is time for everything.

—THOMAS EDISON (1847–1931)

WE LIVE IN A BUSY world, with most of us juggling our family with work, friends, work, exercise, work, bills, emails, and work. It is difficult for us, but our children don't have it easy, either. They are trying to keep up their grades, play sports, be involved with clubs, make friends and fit in, complete their homework, clean their rooms, do their chores, and stay out of trouble. There is so much going on in our lives, and many of us aren't taking the time to relax and find a way to create a reasonable balance that will allow us to fit in all the activities we want to be involved with. This can be especially bad for teachers and parents, because when we aren't able to find a good balance for all we have on our plates, our children are usually the ones who suffer.

Balancing Instruction to Meet Different Learning Styles

During my first year of teaching, I was determined to turn my students into excellent writers. I didn't care if they had to write down to the bone, they were going to become great writers. I would stay up late every night, making corrections to their work. I would sit with the students individually, showing them their mistakes. We wrote, we wrote, we wrote, and in the end their handwriting got much, much better. For the most part, however, the content did not, and at the end of the year the class scored dead last in the county in writing. I didn't understand what I was doing wrong. Mrs. Jones's students, however, had scored second in the county in math. I noticed that she was demonstrating to her students how she would solve problems. She would talk the class through each problem, step by step, showing the students her thought process and how she came up with her answer. I thought that if it worked for math, it would work for writing as well.

At the beginning of the next school year I made overheads that just had lines on them, and each day I devoted a portion of class time to writing. Whatever the students' assignment, I would take the same task and show them how I would respond in writing. I talked through the process, explaining the importance of the opening sentence, how I was avoiding repetition throughout, trying to keep it entertaining, and all the while maintaining the structure. This process grew, and soon instead of writing *for* the students, I was writing *with* the students. I would ask for suggestions as I wrote on the overhead, and the students would speak up if they had an idea. They didn't raise their hands, they just spoke out their ideas—never shouting them, just making comments and giving suggestions. I would pick out good ideas from the group and say, "Oh, I like that," and I would write it down. I seldom had to stop because the students were so full of ideas and the writing just flowed. Soon the students' own writing began to flourish. I would remove the names from their papers, make overheads of their writing, and share it with the entire class. We would point out the negatives and positives of each piece and give suggestions on how it could be improved. After showing the students my writing, they improved because they had an example to learn from, but when I showed them the writing of their peers, they seemed to enjoy that even more and they made outstanding improvements. We soon started to grade the papers on a four-point scale, and after much practice, the students were allowed to grade each other's papers. I would place the students in groups of four, and the students would take turns reading and grading the papers. I would then join each group and listen as they discussed their reasons for their grades and how each paper could be made better.

For about three-quarters of the writing assignments I

had the students do only a first draft. One of the comments I heard at the beginning of the year was that the students hated writing because they had to do revision after revision until it was perfect. I didn't want the students to get so aggravated and consumed with one piece of writing, so I just let them have fun with it, writing something only once and placing a great deal of effort into getting it right the first time. I found that by doing it that way, the students were able to get a lot more practice with writing and enjoyed the process much more. There were some assignments that we would revise and really polish up, but that was less common.

By the end of the year when we took our writing tests, the students scored first in the county. It wasn't because they had been writing, writing, writing but because they had been exposed to writing in many different ways, using all different types of techniques. They had seen me write; we wrote together as a class; they had learned how to grade writing; they had scored each other's papers; they had discussed their work; they wrote in all different types of genres and on every subject; and they had learned to enjoy expressing themselves through their words.

This approach to learning needs to be applied in every subject. Kids learn differently; some are visual learners, some respond better to things they hear, and others respond to things they experience. Some kids focus best when they are in quiet surroundings; others enjoy reading while listening to U2 and watching MTV at the same time. It is important as teachers and parents for us to present information to students in many different ways so that we are covering all the bases and reaching all the children.

Mrs. Jones still teaches in Aurora, and each year she has over 90 percent of her students testing on grade level in math. The reason for this is that she presents the information in a balanced way, covering all different types of learning styles. She has the students working with manipulative items, in groups, on the computers, in their books, and on the overhead; they are out of their seats, discovering math around the school, and sometimes working silently or with a partner. She presents all the problems in many different ways, showing the students many avenues to take in order to find the solution. She encourages every student to tackle the problems in the way that makes sense to them and to use the strategy they are most comfortable with. It's that type of instruction that we must present to our students.

When I taught in New York City and was trying to reach the needs of thirty-seven students in one class, I felt as if I was going to lose it. I never felt that I was doing an adequate job. One technique I used that seemed to work, however, involved having the students participate in an activity I called "Musical Marathon." I would greet my students in the hall and tell them that they were about to embark on a mission of magnificent proportions. I would tell them that there are three rules:

1. They must, above all else, work with their team members. I would mention a few words about working together and supporting ideas.

2. If they hear music, they have three seconds to become silent, and anyone who speaks after that time while the music is playing will lose points for their team.

3. When they hear music, after they become completely silent they must quietly move to the set of desks to their left.

That is it. No more rules. I would then begin to play music, the students would become silent and then walk into the room. There they would see that I had the desks divided into seven groups. On each set of desks there were name cards showing the students where to sit. In the center of each set of desks was an assignment that the group had to complete in seven minutes. I would turn off the music, and off to work they would go. At the end of seven minutes I played the music again and gave the students seven seconds to get to the next group of desks to their left. For the next hour, the teams would make their way around the room until they had completed each assignment.

The first time I did this with the students was a learning process. Some teams took forever to change groups, some didn't work together, and some were constantly looking to remember everything she taught us about that night and all the surrounding events of the Revolutionary War. I can remember standing there in front of the class reciting the verses. I can see Melanie Ebron sitting there, staring at me through those thick glasses with that smug look on her face. She had said every single line, and I was trying to sort through whether it was the Old North Arch or the Belfry Church or how many lanterns were in that tower, and it was a mess. Still, I got through it, and having to recite that poem and all I learned during that time have stayed with me.

In today's education there doesn't seem to be much weight given to getting kids to memorize information. With the Internet and calculators, everything they could ever want is at their fingertips, so there is little need for them to memorize anything. In some schools, teachers are even spending very little time teaching the multiplication tables because calculators are so prevalent, and they feel there is little need for mental math. Everyone is devoting time to teaching kids how to do research and how to find the answers to their questions. I agree that giving students those skills is important, and we must help them to be self-sufficient and give them the tools to research and to be lifelong learners. In addition, however, we must prepare our students to think for themselves and have a wealth of knowledge already within them that they can draw from.

With many of the lessons I teach, I try to have my students involved with something they have to memorize. I me for advice, which I wouldn't give them. I wanted them to learn to work together, and, more important, I wanted them to participate in all the different types of learning styles that were presented.

One activity had a tape recording with ear phones for each student. The night before, I had read different parts of a story on each tape; and each student would be listening to a different part. Each student had to listen carefully because no one else was hearing their part of the story. In the center of the desks was a sheet with twenty-five questions that required the information each person had learned in order to answer.

Another section had measuring tape and eight boxes, some small, some large, that I had gathered from around the school. I had taped a number, 1 to 8, on each box, and the students had to list the area of each one, in inches, on a sheet of paper.

I borrowed a set of encyclopedias from another teacher and had them in one section. On a sheet of paper I had listed thirty famous scientists, and the students had to match them with their accomplishments that were listed on the right side of the page.

In another section the students had to weigh twenty objects and list their weight in grams. In another they had to use tangrams in order to solve a puzzle. Each time we played "Musical Marathon" I had different activities depending on what we were learning. No matter what the students were required to do, however, having them involved with hands-on activities and having them learn to work together and actually apply the things they were learning in class really helped them connect with what we were learning.

When I think of classrooms where the students sit in the same place every day and the teachers lecture on and on, it breaks my heart. When we are working with kids, we have to find ways to present information in ways that the students enjoy, and, even more important, we have to make sure that we are using a balanced approach toward education and addressing all the different learning levels and styles that are present in the children.

Finding the Right Balance with Discipline and Love

I have heard from many teachers who are using the rules listed in *The Essential 55* in their classrooms. Most have broken down the list into a number that works for them, whether it is twenty or forty, but some have used all fifty-five. And when I say all fifty-five, I mean all fifty-five, even the joking rule about "No Doritos." I visited one school where they had outlawed Doritos entirely.

Most of the teachers and parents I have heard from have said the rules are really working well. Some have said, however, that they are having problems getting their students to accept so many rules. In reality, you can have 1,000 rules and it still won't matter unless you have a good relationship with the students. There must be a balance. You have to be firm and you have to be consistent, but at the same time you can't be so strict that the students rebel and don't want to please you. On the other hand, you can't spend all your time trying to get the students to like you, because even if they do like you, in the end they won't respect you and will probably end up running over you. There has to be a balance. The discipline must be in place, and you have to show the kids that you care about them and find ways to make them like being around you and in your class.

This also goes for parents. I have seen parents who are too strict with their children, and the kids end up acting out, not doing well in school, smoking, talking back, or using any other way they can to rebel. When there is a strong relationship between the parents and their children, this happens much less often. On the other hand, some parents avoid discipline because they don't want to strain their relationship with their child. They will sometimes give punishments but will soon relent under pressure from the child. Children raised in that type of environment learn not to respect authority. They learn from their parents that words have no real meaning and their actions have no true consequences. With children it's all about finding a balance. You have to maintain discipline and be consistent. You must mean what you say and stick to it. If you know you really aren't going to enforce a whole week without TV, then don't say there will be no TV for a week. It is much more powerful to give a realistic punishment and stick to it than to give a punishment that sounds really powerful and bad at the time but ends up not really being as severe as you claimed. Parents also need to make sure that the relationship with their children is strong. If children look up to their parents and enjoy being around them, they will be far more likely to respect them and adhere to their wishes. Children who learn at a young age not to obey authority will become teenagers who talk back, act out, and are disrespectful.

My parents always did a good job of giving realistic punishments, and when they said it, I knew they meant it. At the same time my parents never yelled or said negative things toward me. They were supportive and loving. Their best quality, however, was their humor. When I was growing up, they would make me laugh so hard with their facial expressions, clever wit, classic one-liners, and humorous take on the world. Anyone who knows my parents has cracked up in laughter more than once. That humor, mixed with their kindness, support, and love, is why I respected them. I didn't want to let them down, and when they had to enforce discipline, my sister, Tassie, and I both listened. It is that type of balance that needs to be in place. Parents have to be fun, kind, and supportive, and people their child wants to be around. At the same time they must be consistent and firm.

Balancing Life with Teaching

When I was growing up, I always had a huge amount of energy. I was always running around, going from place to place, person to person, room to room, finding out what was going on and being in the middle of everything. My grandmother, Mudder, who was always quick with her words, used to tell me, "Ron, I think you're afraid someone's going to break wind and you aren't going to smell it."

When I started teaching, I poured all of that energy into the school, my classroom and mainly my students. I would be up until 2:00 A.M. planning lessons, and I would be the first person at school in the morning. I was running full-steam ahead. I was going to change the world, and no one was going to stop me. After about six months, something happened. I was dead. My energy was drained. I was overwhelmed by all that my students needed from me. Paperwork was all over my desk. I just had to get away. I went to visit a friend of mine named Robyn, and she said to me, "Ron, you're burnt out." Then she said something very wise: "Ron, in order to teach about life, you have to have a life."

She was right. I was living at school morning, noon, and night, and it was too much. I was losing myself in the school. When I looked in the mirror, I didn't see Ron, I saw Mr. Clark.

From that moment on I continued to go full-steam

ahead at school and keep that plate quite full, but at the same time I have made time for me, for my friends, and for my family. Sometimes you just have to let things go. I can remember times in North Carolina when I had tons of papers to grade, but my friend Joey would want to play tennis; so I would choose tennis. The next day I would pass back the papers, and we would go over them together in class. I learned quickly that it isn't necessary to grade every single item the students complete, and I realized that by taking the time to play tennis, I got a good workout and ended up sleeping better and feeling more refreshed in the morning. That day when I taught I had more energy, and there was pep in my step.

My first year of teaching I had an after-school Ghost Writer's Club. We would watch the *Ghostwriter* TV show, list clues in our notebooks, and try to solve the mysteries ourselves. The students really looked forward to it, and I never wanted to cancel a meeting. At lunch I was talking with Mrs. Jones, and after I told her how burned out I was and how I wished I didn't have to keep the club students after school that day, she just said, "Mr. Clark, cancel. It's no problem. The students can call their parents now during lunch to let them know, and you won't have to worry about it." She told me that sometimes as teachers we have to allow ourselves to have a break. That is okay, and we cannot feel guilty about it. She was right. That day after the bell I went straight home and took a nap. That night I just watched

TV, kicked back, and chilled. The next morning I was a new person.

Recharging is necessary, and it will make us a better teacher and also a better person. It is important for everyone, not only teachers. On average, Americans have less time off and fewer vacations than any nation in the world. We strive for success and focus on output, and oftentimes we sacrifice our health and emotional well-being to meet the needs of the job.

At times, it seems we are even more concerned with products than we are with people. I can remember as a little boy watching how my grandparents and aunts and uncles interacted with everyone. They seemed to be so close and really have strong bonds. People took time to sit and talk, to rest with one another on the porch, to share parts of themselves, and to learn from one another. Now it seems as if most human interaction is done via emails and instant messaging, and the time we spend with our friends and loved ones is minimal. That is a shame, and if we are going to truly find a balance that offers us the greatest happiness, we must find a way to make time for the ones we love and care for in our lives. Having a strong unit of friends and family will contribute to the mind, body, and soul, and fulfill our lives and make us better workers and happier people.

When we are given the choice between work and our loved ones, sometimes we must make the sacrifices for ourselves, and we can't feel guilty about it. We have to find a balance between work and our lives outside of work; otherwise, we will burn out so much quicker and then not have the energy or desire to stay in the profession long enough to make a lasting contribution.

6. COMPASSION

*An understanding heart is everything in a
teacher, and cannot be esteemed highly enough. One
looks back with appreciation to the brilliant teachers,
but with gratitude to those who touched our human
feeling. The curriculum is so much necessary raw
material, but warmth is the vital element for the
growing plant and for the soul of the child.*

—CARL JUNG (1875–1961)

MORE AND MORE IT SEEMS that compassion is missing from our society, and many children are growing up with a lack of consideration for others. It is important
that all of us—parents, teachers, and other members of the
community—treat others with compassion, consideration,
and generosity, especially children. When we show kindness
to a child, we are doing more than passing on a good deed.
We are building a vision in the eyes of that child of how
others should be treated. When we as teachers, parents, and
members of law enforcement, day care, and other service categories treat children in a way that belittles them, lets them

down, or affects them negatively, we are instilling in those children a stereotype of what is expected from different members of society.

I have met a lot of students across the country, and one of my favorite questions to ask them is "Why do you like your teacher?" Over half of the students respond, "She/he is kind to me." We can never underestimate the power of kindheartedness and treating our children with consideration. Most children wear their hearts on their sleeve, and if we want them to trust and respect us, we must take care not to treat them in any way that is negative or hurtful.

Putting Yourself in Someone Else's Shoes

Ramon . . . Rrramon . . . Rrrrrrrramon. . . . Rrrrrrrrrrrrra-mon? . . . Those words still haunt me.

When I was a freshman in high school, my family moved from Chocowinity to Belhaven, a town located across the county. As far as I was concerned, it might as well have been on the other side of the world, because I had to leave all my friends and my hometown. The worst part was that I was going to attend a new school. It was situated next to a crab house, and on Tuesdays and Thursdays the entire school reeked of crab. Even worse than the smell was the fact that I knew absolutely no one, and I was scared to death.

I was placed in a Spanish II class with all seniors. I was small, skinny, pale, and nervous, and the senior football jocks were seated all around me. My Spanish name was "Ramon," and throughout class the boys would begin to whisper "Ramon," "Rrrramon," "Rrrrrrramon" over and over, day after day. They would call my name and laugh under their breath. The redder my face turned, the louder they became. I can remember looking at the teacher, Señor Walhamb, begging him with my eyes to do something. The fear within my heart was so great that I never would have asked for help. I was afraid that if I tattled, I would endure something even more painful and torturous than the grief I was experiencing every day in fifth period. I didn't want to find out what would happen if I ratted out the "kings" of the school. It got to the point where I wouldn't even eat lunch because I was so worried about the coming class.

Now when I look back, it all seems so foolish. I should have turned around in the middle of class and said, "What? Can I help you?" I was losing sleep. My grades in that class were horrible—A's in all the others, but C's and D's in that class. I should have let Señor Walhamb know. Then again, as I recall, he already knew. He heard it every day. He just looked at the boys and frowned and went about his business. As teachers we must be aware of the climate of our classrooms and how the students are interacting with one another. We have to make sure that our students feel safe and comfortable and that they are able to focus on their education.

I can easily recall the emotions I encountered in that

class throughout the year. Unfortunately, there are kids in classrooms all across America going through the same type of torture. I was actually a popular student. I often played the role of class clown, and I was never short of friends. With that said, if I was miserable and was being bullied, I can only imagine how students who struggle in school and who are not surrounded by friends manage to succeed at all. No wonder so many of our students are dropping out and saying they absolutely hate school.

Every year I make a point to tell my students about that time when I was bullied and how it made me feel. It is my hope that by expressing my feelings and the pain I went through I will help them realize how they make other students feel when they pick on them, call them names, or use other forms of embarrassment. It isn't comfortable for me to share times that were humiliating, but I have found that it helps. Students in my classes who normally pick on others have started to make an effort to be nicer to their classmates. Even more important, however, I can see how some of my students are able to relate to my stories and how they appreciate knowing there are others who have experienced what they are going through.

Good teachers and parents help kids place themselves in another's shoes in order to see situations from different vantage points. Once kids understand and realize the feelings and emotions of others, they are much more willing to respect those who are different from them.

✒ Teaching Children to Be Compassionate

In East Harlem I taught a self-contained class of thirty-seven students. If they had all been angels, it still would have been a daunting task, but unfortunately there were several students who presented multiple disciplinary problems. There were times when I wanted to pull my hair out, but, surprisingly, the majority of the problems weren't between me and the students, they were between the students themselves. I constantly had to act as a mediator of disagreements, many of which involved every student in the class. Sometimes when rifts arise in the classroom, kids take sides and divide the class into two or three cliques to wage battle, throw insults, and make threats. It can be a nightmare. It is unfair to say this happens only with children, because I am sure if you placed thirty-seven adults in a classroom for 180 days a year, a good share of disagreements would arise. It is only natural for humans to have issues and find grievance with one another. When those issues arise, however, it is important to take the time to teach students how to solve the problems amiably and in a mature manner. When kids are gathered together to discuss the issues and everyone states his or her opinion and view of the problem, a solution usually becomes a simple task. About 90 percent of the time disagreements can be resolved by doing the following:

1. Find out the source of the problem. (Usually there are two main students, often former friends, who are upset with each other.)

2. Get the two students to sit down and talk through the problem.

   KEY QUESTIONS:
   What did Sheila do that upset you?
   Tell Shelia and me what you think happened.
   How did what happened make you feel?
   What could Sheila do that would make you
     feel better?

I would also ask Sheila the same questions.

3. Show the rest of the class that the two girls have resolved their problem. If appropriate, I ask them to sit together at lunch or I put them on a project together. I try to show the rest of the class that all animosity is over so that they will jump off the bandwagon and things can return to normal.

4. Tell the students the issue will not be discussed again. If I hear any of the students bringing up the matter, I tell them I will punish them in the same way as if they were at the center of the altercation.

5. Talk to the students about how the situation could have been resolved before it blew out of proportion. Whenever possible it is good to give the kids tools they can use themselves so that similar problems won't arise in the future.

Maintaining order in the classroom and helping kids get along and show compassion for one another can be difficult, and dealing with bullies and "friends" at school who turn against each other is tricky. Part of our job as teachers and parents is to be aware of bullying issues or problems in the classroom. Many kids will keep quiet because they are afraid of being embarrassed or making the bully even angrier. They will keep what is going on bottled up inside them, and unless we take notice, we might never realize what is going on. There are some things we as parents and teachers can do to learn whether children are being bullied.

PARENTS

Monitor your child's friends • If your child no longer mentions his or her friends or becomes defensive when you ask why he doesn't talk with a certain friend anymore, this may be a sign that something has happened. You know your child's communication style best. Watch for any changes in the way friends are referred to.

Watch for changes in grades • If your child has a sudden drop in grades, this could be a sign of the pressure he is experiencing at school. Also, if your child changes classes and there is a sudden drop in the grades in one subject, there could be students in that class who are giving your child problems.

Make sure your child isn't excluded • If your child doesn't have a solid group of friends to hang out with and depend on and if your child isn't involved in any clubs, this could be a sign he is isolated and picked on at school. If my child were in this situation, I would try to figure out why he was being excluded. Sometimes when children have personalities, hobbies, or interests that are different from the rest of the class, they can find it hard to fit in. Because of those differences, they can also be bullied. In this case I would try to get my child involved in a club or association where he could find children with similar interests. If he did develop a friendship, I would make every effort to get them together— at the movies or on family trips. My nephew Austin is eight, and when he plays with other kids his age, they mostly just want to wrestle and play video games. Recently, however, he was playing with his cousin Dylan, and they played for four hours with a science kit. I told his mom, "We have to get these two together more often."

It's important for parents to help their children form bonds with other kids who will have a positive influence. It is also important for teachers to try to help kids who seem isolated. In New York City I had one student who was extremely bright, but she was quiet and didn't have many friends. I took her and another girl out of class and asked them to be involved in a huge science project, letting them know they would have to work together outside of school. Soon they were spending every Saturday at each other's homes working on the project. They started eating together at lunch and became great friends. Sometimes we just have to keep our eyes open and give a little push when the time comes.

On a side note, some kids are more comfortable in small groups and not every child feels the need to have a multitude of friends, but I think it is a shame to allow a child to grow up without peers whom he feels a bond with and whom he can confide in.

TEACHERS

Do not *ignore any signs of bullying in your school* • There is a lot to be said for allowing children to handle issues on their own, and it is important to spend time working with kids to get them to settle disputes and disagreements; however, when that doesn't work, it is time to take charge. I have been there; I have felt the pain of being picked on and being bullied, and it is a living nightmare for a child. Don't let it go on in front of you without doing something about it.

Do not *make the situation worse* • As a male teacher I was always being asked to go into the boys' restroom to break up fights and the occasional game of toilet tissue basketball. One day I went in to find two boys, James and Jegonda, fighting. Jegonda was unusually tall for fourth grade, and his neck was very long. He told me that James had been saying he looked like a dinosaur, so they were fighting. I was on the way with my class to the cafeteria; I dropped the two boys off at their classroom and told the teacher what had happened. In front of the entire class she said, "Oh, I don't doubt they were fighting. James and the other kids keep calling him Jegonda-saur because he is tall and dark-skinned." She then turned to the students and said that she was taking recess away from the entire class for three days because she was tired of Jegonda's being picked on. I was standing beside Jegonda, and I know he must have wanted to just disappear. I could see on his face that he was mortified as the entire class started to moan and complain about the punishment he was sure to be blamed for.

As teachers and parents we have to remember that the emotions of children are very different from ours, and what might seem to us like something that should be shrugged off or ignored isn't so easily handled by our students. When we encounter situations that involve bullies and kids who are being picked on, we have to do whatever is possible not to create more damage and make matters worse. When I am in a situation where I know a child is being victimized,

the first thing I do is sit down with him after school or during lunch to find out exactly what is going on and who is
picking on him. I had a situation with a child named Sara.
When I sat down and asked her who was picking on her,
she said, "Everyone." When something like that happens,
there is a need to address the entire class, but in order to do
that, the affected child should not be present. Jegonda's
teacher humiliated him without even knowing it.

In Sara's situation, I sent her and three girls I knew
weren't involved with picking on her to help a teacher in
another room for a class period. I then went about teaching
my lesson, and in the middle I stopped and said, "You know,
that reminds me of something I have been meaning to talk
to you about." I then brought up the topic of how we treat
one another in our class and how it feels to be made fun of. I
never mentioned Sara's name, but I encouraged everyone to
be kind to one another with no name calling or picking on
others in any way. I then asked them to go out of their way
to be kind to others in the class whom they might not usually be kind to. And finally I reminded them that it was okay
not to like everyone in the class, because throughout life
they are not going to like everyone they meet, but it is crucial to treat everyone with respect and kindness nonetheless.
All of that came with a final stern comment about how anyone who is found picking on others in any way will have to
face the consequences. You can get a good two weeks' worth
of peace out of a talk like that.

In the meantime, I wanted to find a way to help Sara make friends. In her case, she was often called "stupid" because of her low grades. I called her into class early for a few days to work on a writing assignment. We went over her writing and then at home she worked on the revisions. Soon it was perfect, and I then gave the entire class the same assignment. When I handed back the papers, I told the students that one of the completed assignments showed great merit. I always make a big production about work that shows great improvement or achievement. I read a paragraph from the paper, and all the students clapped in approval. I then said, "And this paper, with a score of one hundred, goes to . . . Sara McDonnel." There was a gasp and then a round of applause from the class. Step one of my plan was in motion.

That afternoon I gave Sara a list of three mind problems that dealt with math and science and the techniques for solving them. I told her to come in early the next morning if she had any questions, and she did. We went over them for a few minutes, and she finally understood them. The next day at the end of math class I said, "And now I have a possible treat for you. I have written three problems on the board. I want you all to work silently for five minutes to come up with the answers, and then I am going to call one of you up to the front of the class to complete the problems. If that person gets them all correct, the entire class does not have to do this extra homework worksheet." I then reminded them that they should work extremely hard for the next five minutes because they did not know who would be called up. I have a container with my students' names, and when the five minutes were up, I reached my hand inside and said, "Okay, the student who can possibly win you all a free homework pass is Sara McDonnel." Now, I have a rule in my class that there is to be no moaning whatsoever, so not a sound was made, but I could tell there was a moan-fest of massive proportions going on inside those kids. Sara walked to the front of the room and with great ease solved the three problems. When she was done, I announced, "Sara McDonnel has just given the entire class a free homework pass for the night!" Everyone cheered and gave her high-fives as she walked back to her seat. A few days earlier she had sat with me, crying that everyone hated her and picked on her. Now she had become the class hero. The influence a teacher can have on a classroom and on changing situations like that can be enormous.

Don't be afraid to show compassion • I am an extremely strict teacher and demand a lot of my students in terms of behavior and class work, but I want them to know the reason I set my expectations so high is that I care about them and want them to get the best education possible and be able to choose the future they would like to have. I also do things for my students, such as bake cookies, cheer them on, visit their homes, attend their games, and be there for them when they need me. Doing so much outside of the classroom isn't realistic in most situations, but showing compassion can be accomplished just by the way we treat our students and the things we say to them. Letting the students know that you care about them breaks down a lot of doors and goes a long way toward getting them to perform the way you want. The best way to create compassion within the classroom is to model that type of behavior yourself.

Create an environment from day one that sets the tone in your classroom • I greet my students on the first day of school by saying, "This year we are going to be a family. We are going to work together, support one another, and treat one another with respect. The one thing I will not tolerate this year is bullying or picking on other students in this classroom. That is something I take very seriously, and it will definitely not be happening in this classroom."

As with many issues concerning classroom management and discipline, it is always best to start off on the right foot and lay the groundwork for the year ahead. It is a great idea to mention on day one how you feel about bullying and what the classroom protocols will be for dealing with such behavior.

✎ Kids Who Are Bullies: Kids Who Lack Compassion for Other Students

Handling one incident of bullying is one thing, but doing something to make sure it doesn't happen again is another.

Usually, if a student begins to bully others, that behavior will continue for many years. Therefore, we need to do what we can to stop it when it starts to occur and prevent it from happening again. One of the best things we can do is let the parents know what is going on, because in most cases the reason a child is bullying others can be traced back to the home. Some of the reasons that kids begin to bully others are these:

They are not getting enough attention from their parents.

They witness adults in their home handle situations with violence and in an aggressive manner, thereby learning how to exercise authority and state their beliefs through intimidation and force.

They are insecure and try to point out the weaknesses of others in order to feel better about themselves.

They are trying to fit in. By making their peers laugh, usually at the expense of other students, they feel as though they are being accepted.

They want to have friends and are trying to do so through intimidation. They feel others will be nice to them because they will be afraid of what would happen if they don't.

They are taking out their anger on other students. Usually kids whose parents are going through a divorce or who are having to deal with issues in the home will bottle up their anger, fear, and true feelings on the matter. While at school, and without even realizing they are doing so, they will take that anger out on other students.

If you feel there are issues within the home that are causing problems that are too intricate for you to handle, it is a good idea to recommend that the child speak with a counselor to try to uncover the true cause of the behavior. I know if I were a principal I would beg my counselors to focus on the bullies and the reasons for their behavior. One student can often be the catalyst for multiple problems, and by dealing with their needs a lot of other issues will be avoided.

Compassion for the Elderly

I was fortunate that my grandmother lived with us during my childhood. I had a very strong bond with her, and I grew to respect the challenges of the elderly and to admire the wisdom acquired over their many years. It was heartbreaking when my grandmother, Mudder, got to the point where she needed assistance walking and doing other normal chores that the proud woman usually did herself. Watching age take away the gifts of youth is a difficult experience, but because I saw it firsthand, I grew to have a heightened respect for the elderly. As adults we tend to respect those who remind us of those we have formed bonds with in the past. Every time I see an elderly woman in the grocery store, on a bus, or elsewhere, I see my grandmother. Out of respect for her memory, I treat that person with kindness and patience. My father used to drive like a madman, speeding here and speeding there. Now that he isn't as young as he used to be, he drives at a slower pace and with much more caution. When I am driving and am behind an extremely slow car, instead of getting upset or letting it bother me, I imagine that the driver is similar to my father, whose reflexes are not what they used to be, who is wisely taking it slower.

In our society, children seem to have less and less respect for others, especially adults. I think the main reason for this is that they aren't forming bonds with adults as they used to. They have less of a connection to others and are more likely to be rude or disrespectful. Kids used to be raised to respect their grandparents and the elderly. That doesn't seem to be stressed now, and our society is becoming centered on the fast, devoted to the young, and embarrassed by the old.

There are many things teachers can do to help prevent that from happening, and it is important to point out that the elderly we ignore today will become the reality we experience tomorrow. One suggestion for teachers is to have older individuals come into the classroom to talk about their experiences and different areas of expertise. I have had individuals come in who served in wars, were active during the Civil Rights movement, and who have traveled all over the world. They always offered a great deal of wonderful information for the students, but they also showed the students that being old doesn't mean being boring and that the exterior of a person can in no way measure the life that is inside.

Instead of having a person visit the class, it also works well to have the students interview their neighbors or grandparents. When I was in high school, I was given an assignment to interview someone who lived during the Great Depression. I selected my grandmother, Mudder, and as I asked her question after question, I was shocked to hear her answers. I had never taken the time to discuss what her life was like when she was growing up, and I never knew of the struggles and sacrifices she experienced. It was an eye-opening event for me, and it drew me much closer to Mudder.

Some schools visit rest homes, adopt grandparents, deliver baked goods, help the elderly shop for groceries, and participate in a number of other programs. What is important is that through these efforts students begin to realize how the elderly in our society should be honored, appreciated, and respectfully treated.

Compassion for Everyone

One of the lessons I always try to teach my students is not to see a person's exterior self only. I tell them to look within and judge that person by what is inside. I have said a million times, "It's okay not to like someone. We are only human, and that is natural. But don't have negative thoughts or opinions about a person until you have gotten to know him. After that, if you still don't like him, that is understandable, but not to make the attempt leads you to make a prejudiced judgment." I also add that even though we don't like someone, it is still important to treat that person with respect. Saying those words and getting children to understand them is very important, but it doesn't resolve all the incorrect images and opinions children have of others. We must all go out of our way to treat the youth of today with compassion, support, and love. In that way we will raise a society that has a greater respect for all.

Compassion in the Classroom Can Empower Victimized Students

Many students aren't achieving their potential because they don't see the classroom as a comfortable place where they can learn at ease. When the right type of environment is created, however, those students can flourish and achieve what would not have been possible otherwise. A student of mine named Rubina in New York City was picked on because of her nationality. She was very withdrawn and would never speak out. After months of working with that class, encouraging them to support one another, to lift one another up, and show compassion for their classmates, the class started to change. It didn't happen overnight, and it took many long talks and lots of reinforcement, but if you let the class know of your expectations and if you stick to it, eventually you can create a climate where the students are getting along, respecting each other, and no longer picking on one another.

Each year I installed the following rules in my class:

—If someone does well, we will all clap for that person. We actually practice cheering for each other.

—No negative comments will ever be made about a person's appearance.

—If someone is eating alone at lunch, ask them to join your conversation.

—Never laugh at the misfortune of others. It will find its way back to you.

—Say "good morning" and "see you tomorrow" to each other.

—Never use nicknames. You can only address a person by his first name.

I enforced those rules, and many more, and by November the climate of the class had started to change and that student, Rubina, was starting to speak out. And when she did, the class would cheer and clap, as they did for all students who made contributions to the class. She started to hold her head higher, to smile, to laugh, and to apply herself. In February we had class elections, and Rubina ran for president. She gathered a committee, made the most beautiful posters, passed out buttons with her picture on them, and gave a wonderful speech in front of the entire class. She was running against Derrick, however, the most popular student in the class, and even though he had put up only one poster and laughed through his whole speech, I had a strong feeling he would win. That afternoon I read the votes and made the announcement that Rubina was our new class president. Derrick admitted, with his wide smile and in total honesty, that even he had voted for her, and I believed it. She deserved it, and everyone, even Derrick, knew it.

At the end of the year during our class awards ceremony, Rubina was named class valedictorian. She had achieved a perfect score on her end-of-grade state math test. As I gave her the award, tears rolled down the face of her father, who was sitting over to the side. Her entire family cheered with pride.

That is the type of transformation that can happen when the teacher creates an environment where the students feel comfortable, safe, and supported, and receive the encouragement of their peers. Again, it doesn't happen overnight, but with the right amount of reinforcement and with plenty of good talks and clear guidelines, the class will come around and all the students will be much more productive.

In the normal classroom environment, students generally know the teacher wants to help them and wants them to learn, but they feel that the rest of the class doesn't really care how they perform. And in most cases, unfortunately, the rest of the class really *doesn't* care how they perform. Basically, the student is trying to please his teacher, his parents, and himself. If teachers can find a way, however, to place compassion in the classroom and get the students to show interest in one another's work and care about one another, that gives each child the knowledge that about twenty-five more people care about her success. I really build it up big in my class, and I tell them that if we are going to be the best possible class, then it is going to take every one of us to achieve that. I say that not only does each one of us have to reach the top, but we must also make sure we are taking our classmates with us. I say, "Everyone in here has a strength, and everyone in here has a weakness. We can all contribute, and we can all help one another. Let's work together, pull one another up, support one another, and shoot for the moon!" Again, this isn't a quick transformation, but over time you will start to see a big change in your students. They will want to do well for themselves and will feel part of a class that is like a team, where everyone cares about them and wants to see them succeed.

✎ Compassion Can Lead to Understanding

There are two books I like to read with my students that I would recommend that all teachers and parents use with their children. Both books have similar titles and, in my opinion, a similar message. They are appropriate for ages seven to thirteen, though as an adult, I love them, too. The first one is *The Hundred Dresses,* by Eleanor Estes, which is about a poor girl who moves to a new school and tells the other students that even though she wears rags, she has one hundred beautiful dresses in her closet. The students know she is lying, and they pick on her and call her names constantly. In the end, the girl moves away, and the children in the class find out that she did have one hundred beautiful dresses—but they were just drawings the girl had done of the dresses she envisioned in her mind. I love discussing this book with kids because it covers many levels: accepting children who are different, explaining why someone might be dishonest, the emotions of a new student, not making quick judgments about others. It touches on several topics and really helps students see the point of view of others.

Another book that deals with compassion is *The Hundred Penny Box* by Sharon Bell Mathis. It is about an elderly lady who keeps one hundred pennies in a box, one penny for each year of her life. Throughout the book she tells her grandson, Michael, the meaning of each penny and stories that go along with it. Anyone who has an elderly grand-mother can relate to this story, but it is also good for kids who don't have a close relationship with an elderly person. It helps to show them that even though someone might be old, he or she once lived with vitality and spirit, just like a kid. It also shows them that each elderly person has a wealth of experiences, heartache, love, wisdom, and memories, and that out of admiration for the long life the person has led, each elderly person should be cherished and respected.

Showing Compassion with Patience

When dealing with children, one of the best ways to show compassion is to have patience. When a person is trying to learn something new or attempt something that is unfamil-iar to them or difficult, it is hard enough without having to deal with a frustrated and impatient adult. In order to make children feel more comfortable it is best to do whatever it takes to refrain from showing irritation, annoyance, or aggravation.

When I was teaching in New York City my class was given a set of laptops from the district, and we were all thrilled. There were problems, however, because I had thirty-seven students and there were only twenty-four laptops. Most of the students had to pull their desks together and share, and there was already a lack of space in the room, and it made us all more cramped than usual. In addition, there were cords and plugs running all over the room, and I had to set up the big LCD projector in the middle of the room so I could demonstrate for the students on the overhead screen.

The first day we started using the computers, I was at my wits' end. I was frustrated and overwhelmed by the logistics of simply setting up all the computers. Two of the laptops didn't work, many of the students didn't follow the directions and ended up opening incorrect programs, it took Tamara five minutes before her computer ended up on the floor, and we were all a bit tense and uncomfortable. We decided to put away the computers and try again the next day.

I decided to approach the laptops knowing that there were going to be issues and to just Take It Slow, Go Step by Step, and Expect the Unexpected. We started off the day by discussing maintenance issues such as how to handle the computers properly and how to turn them on correctly. I demonstrated at the front of the room before I allowed the students to get their own laptops. We then organized a system for distributing the computers so that there was no chaos or disorder. We didn't want to take the chance of anyone bumping into each other and dropping a computer . . . again.

When we started getting into the programs, I kept the attitude that this was going to be a long process and that it would take a lot of review and patience. Even when I had over half the class on the wrong screen, I would just talk in a calm and understanding manner and lead everyone to the right screen. I mentioned to the class that this was going to be a bit challenging for all of us for a while, and that in order to avoid frustration we should all be quiet, pay attention, and give our best efforts to following the directions carefully.

Over time, the students began to really catch on, and before I knew it they were navigating all over the computers with ease, and they loved it. They had been apprehensive at first, but by taking it slow and encouraging them along the way, they began to feel comfortable and they started to really enjoy the laptops. Many of the students advanced so fast that they were teaching me things and instead of me giving support they were helping each other. If I had acted annoyed or like I was aggravated with the students in the beginning, many of them may not have ever gotten to a point where they were comfortable and confident in using the laptops.

Taking that type of attitude with children is essential whether you are a teacher or a parent. One of the most stressful situations ever is tutoring a kid or helping a kid with his homework in a one-on-one situation. It can be slow, tiring, and exasperating. Parents and teachers should just enter that experience knowing that it is going to be time-consuming and at times a struggle. They should remain positive and never become negative or pessimistic throughout the entire time. I have seen some parents lose their patience when working with children, and from then on out it is like pulling teeth to get the kids to sit down and do the work each night. If I knew I was going to be fussed at or that my parent was going to become angry, I certainly would want to avoid that at all costs. Parents who are pleasant, calm, and encouraging create a type of environment where kids feel free to attempt the work without fear or uneasiness. They enjoy their parents' support, and doing the homework together is seen as a positive experience.

In the classroom, teachers should show that same type of patience. When asking a student a question, don't be so quick to move on to another child if the first student doesn't answer immediately. Some kids will know the answer; it just takes them a while to formulate a response. When I encounter students like that, I just picture that they are my own child or my niece or nephew. I certainly wouldn't want a teacher to damage their self-esteem by moving on so quickly. I would want him or her to be patient and give the child the chance to respond.

Teachers should also let their students' mastery of knowledge guide the curriculum. I have seen teachers who are bound and determined to get through the entire textbook, and they stick to the schedule no matter what. It is far more effective to monitor the students' progress and go at a pace that works for them. All students learn at different rates, and if you have a class that isn't retaining the information you are presenting, it doesn't matter how much is covered, because they still won't grasp the concepts. Teaching faster doesn't necessarily mean the students will learn more. It is necessary to make sure that the students are mastering the material before presenting them with new concepts.

7. CONFIDENCE

*Whether you believe you can do a thing
or not, you are right.*

—HENRY FORD (1863–1947)

HALF OF THE BATTLE in raising kids is teaching them to be confident. Anyone who has ever been successful had to take some risks and experience adversity along the way. In order to face those challenges, children need to have the confidence to feel that they can and will be successful. There are so many individuals out there who have the potential for greatness but never use their abilities for fear of failure or because they don't believe in themselves. All parents and teachers should work to ensure that doesn't occur in the lives of our children.

Experience Leads to Confidence

This is an obvious one. The more children experience a certain situation, the more they are going to become able to handle themselves successfully. That is why I travel so much with students and spend so much time placing them in environments that are new to them. This summer I took some of my former fifth graders, now in high school, to Atlanta. While there, we ate at one of the most expensive restaurants, Blue Pointe. I reviewed table manners with the students over and over. I stressed that the first thing the students should do when they sit down is place the napkin in their lap. We entered the restaurant, and when we sat down, waiters and attendants surrounded our table. Numerous glasses and silverware sat before us, and I could see in the students' eyes that they were a bit bewildered. Suddenly I noticed that we didn't have cloth napkins in front of us. The attendants were going to bring them to us and place them in our laps. When I thought to tell the students, however, it was too late. I noticed them looking quite unsure of themselves as they slowly slid the tea cozies off the table and into their laps. It tickled me so much that I just had to put my head down and laugh. I later explained the mistake to the kids, and we all laughed. Moments like that can't be taught. They need to be experienced in real life firsthand. My students and I had an amazing time that night, and when we left the restaurant, one of the girls turned to me and said that during the meal she had felt like a queen. Not only did that night make her feel special, but it also gave her an experience she can draw on anytime she is in a similar situation. Some people say, "Ron, why are you so worried with these kids going to fancy meals and practicing interviews and having those skills when they are only in fifth grade?" I tell them it has to do with building confidence. The more these kids experience, the more self-esteem they will have and the better they will feel about themselves. I don't want my students to be twenty-two years old, go to a job interview, be qualified for the job, but not get the position because they don't know how to hold themselves in a certain way and present themselves in a manner that is professional. I don't want my students to go to the prom or a business dinner and have to look at others to see which utensil to use. I want them to have those skills, to have those experiences under their belts, and to have confidence.

✎ Confidence Comes with Preparation

I say it at least a hundred times during each school year: Preparation is the key to success. I don't think there is any wiser advice I can give my students. No matter what we do in life, the best way to ensure that we will be successful is to make sure we are prepared. From studying for a test to trying out for a basketball team to becoming a doctor, all our goals are within our reach if we are willing to put forth the effort, time, blood, sweat, and tears to achieve our goals.

When I was a junior in high school, I ran for a state officer position in the Future Business Leaders of America club. I had to make a speech in front of more than three thousand students from across the state, and I was scared to death. My campaign manager, Carla Boyette, kept telling me that I was going to be fine and not to be such a wimp about it. I tried to take her advice and muster up the courage and confidence to make my speech. When the time came for me to give my address, Carla approached the podium to announce me. She walked to the center of the stage with her head high, her long golden locks of hair flowing behind her. She was on a mission. She reached the podium, looked out at the audience with her piercing blue eyes, and froze. I have never seen someone stand so still in my entire life. There I was, standing ten feet behind her, waiting to be introduced, and she just completely froze. After about fifteen seconds I walked up to her and pulled her gently by the arm. She sprung to life and walked off the stage. I looked out at everyone and attempted to begin my speech. At one point I was supposed to say, "I have a great deal of experience," and then I was supposed to give examples of offices I had held in the past. It came out more like "I have a great deal of experience that gives me experience that will help with experiences because having experiences is something that will help with all experiences." My eyes were glued on Mrs. Toler, my adviser, and every time I said the word *experience,* I saw her sink a little bit further into her seat.

I did not win the election. It wasn't even close.

Carla and I both learned a lot from that experience. I learned the importance of preparation, and Carla learned that she never wanted to stand before a group again in her life. She never wanted to have that sinking feeling in her stomach again. Unfortunately for Carla, that day would soon come. It was the Miss Independence pageant in our hometown, Belhaven. All the beautiful junior girls were participating, and there was a lot of pressure for her to enter. She resisted, however, because each contestant had to make a speech. In the end she reluctantly entered, and as I stood in the crowd that day, I don't know if anyone was pulling for her more than I was. As the time came for her to make her speech, she approached the podium and froze. Ten seconds passed, and she just stared straight ahead. The crowd started to buzz, and suddenly she looked in my eyes. I was trying my best to encourage her, but then she just ran off the stage. There was a gasp from the audience, but it was drowned out by the cheers when Carla marched back onto the stage carrying her speech in her hands. She stood at the microphone and read her speech. When she was done, she looked at me and smiled as she received a standing ovation. She had found the confidence within herself to overcome her greatest fear, and she was named first runner-up in the Miss Independence pageant.

Carla returned to that stage because she never wanted to experience that feeling of failure again—the feeling that you hadn't given your all, that you had let yourself down. I never wanted to experience the feeling again, either, and I realized that no matter what you are doing in life, if you really want to be successful, you have to prepare over and over to the point where mistakes are not an option. Ever since that conference I have made sure that when I give a speech, I live the experience in my mind dozens of times before actually standing before the crowd. I see the faces of the audience, picture the stage and the arena, feel my fears, and deliver my address. When I finally do make a speech, it is just as I had practiced it in my mind. After practicing so many times I realized that when I have prepared to a point where I have a great deal of confidence, the fear of speaking in front of a group is gone.

My aunt Carolyn has always been scared to death of speaking in front of people, and she came to me for advice when she had to make a speech to her fellow office personnel from across the state. I told her, "Aunt Carolyn, you do not want to walk off that stage and regret that speech and wish you could give it again. Imagine that you already gave the speech and it wasn't good. You probably wish you could do it again. Well, imagine that this is your second chance, and you go up there and give it all you've got." I also told Aunt Carolyn that the key to facing fear is preparation. I encouraged her to learn that speech so that she could give it while watching TV, ironing, and jogging all at the same time. She took my advice, and her speech was a grand success, and to this day Aunt Carolyn has no problem speaking in front of groups of people, and she does it all the time.

We need to teach our kids that whether they are making a science presentation, studying for a test, going out for an athletic team, learning a new game, participating in a play, or attempting to face any challenge they have in life, the key to success is preparation. Learn your information, your role, your speech, your materials, your technique, and your delivery to the point where you have complete confidence in your abilities.

✎ Confidence Grows When Students Are Given a Chance to Succeed

In New York City my sixth graders and I decided to put on a dramatic musical. The kids had a lot of energy and talent, and I wanted to find a way to showcase their abilities and create something wonderful. The first step we took involved auditioning for parts. Almost all the girls wanted the lead female role, and almost all the boys wanted to play the villain. When we began the auditions, a girl in the class, Stephanie, asked me if she could try out for the role of the villain. I told her that the person for that role really needed to be a forceful male. As days went on, I was having a difficult time deciding which boy should play the villain, and I turned it over to the class for a vote. Each boy acted out a scene before the class, and I instructed the students to vote on talent and preparation, not on popularity. When it came time to vote, Stephanie raised her hand and asked if she could audition. I told her again that the role of the villain was for a male, and she said, "Mr. Clark, you always say that you try to treat us all equally. Well, I don't think you are doing that if you aren't even going to allow me to audition." She was right, and I asked her to come up to the front of the class. I handed her a script to read from, but she informed me that she didn't need it. Stephanie was a short, beautiful young girl with flowing brown hair. She had such a pleasant face, but when she turned to the class, her brow was raised, her face was contorted, she opened her mouth with a *roar* and began to sing with a threatening growl.

She was amazing, and we had our villain. We spent over five months practicing after school, making costumes, constructing the set, and preparing for the big event, and in the end the students' performance was so good that schools from around Harlem came to our school to see it. We ended up having to do the performance eleven times. There is no doubt that a major reason for the success was Stephanie and her amazing performance. She was good that first day during the classroom audition, but each and every time she did it, she got better as her confidence increased and she grew into the role.

Every time I hear from Stephanie, she tells me that she has recently been to an audition for one role or another in New York City. Her dream is to become an actress, and without doubt she has the talent, the drive, and the confidence to make it happen. I hate to think what would have happened if I had been so closed-minded and not allowed her to audition. She might have lost her passion for drama and for the performing arts. As parents and teachers, we have to do whatever we can not to dampen the energy, the enthusiasm, and the dreams of our children. Sometimes all it takes is having faith in our students and giving them a chance that will lead to increasing their confidence and helping them believe in their own abilities.

✎ Confidence Leads to Success

In New York City many of my sixth graders had to be interviewed by the junior high schools they were applying for. They were all scared to death, and I told them that we would practice and by the time we were finished, they would walk into those interviews beaming with confidence. I gave the students a list of thirty questions that I felt might be asked in the interview. I told them that it would help if they had already worked through their thoughts and had decided how they felt and what their answers would be. I told them to go over the questions in their minds and to visualize themselves giving their answers. At lunch and at recess they practiced with partners, and soon the students were beginning to feel good about getting the opportunity to give their answers. There was a big chance that none of those thirty questions would be asked, but that wasn't important. What was important was that those students were becoming confident and were looking forward to the interview instead of dreading it. They had thought out how they felt about getting into the new school, why education was important to them, and what they enjoyed the most about learning, and many other topics dealing with education. Instead of going into the interview empty-handed, they were prepared with a wealth of information they had thought out and practiced.

Once all the students had reviewed the questions, I set up a desk in my room and we role-played as if they were at the interview. Each student would walk in from the hall, shake the hands of the interviewing committee, and introduce themselves. They would then sit in an appropriate manner and answer each question professionally. At the end they always asked the committee a question they had prepared, and in closing, they thanked them for taking the time to interview them. They would again shake hands, wish the committee a good day and good luck with the selection process, and exit. Every child who attended the interview was accepted to that school.

When we are confident, we walk with a different air in our step, we hold ourselves with pride, and we perform and achieve at much higher levels. Placing confidence in the hearts and minds of children will lead to increased success with all of their endeavors.

Confidence Builders in the Classroom

The power of a teacher can never be overstated. We have the ability to inspire our students to greatness and truly make them realize their potential. In order to do so, we must use every technique possible to build up their confidence and pride in their abilities.

One of the brightest students I ever taught was a young boy named Melvin. He came from a broken home and had spent his entire life being pulled between different schools, homes, and families. When he first walked into my class, he was very withdrawn, and it was almost impossible to get him involved in the class.

One of my bulletin boards for social studies was called the Pyramid of Pride. It was basically a pyramid of gold construction paper, and I would staple the students' test papers in each position, with the highest score being placed at the very top. When I announced the scores for a test, I would go to the pyramid, and as I said the name and score, I would staple the paper to the board and all the students would cheer. I always started at the bottom of the pyramid, building up anticipation of who had the highest score on the test.

I was going through the process with a test on the history of Egypt, and when I got to the top, I paused and said, "And now, with a perfect score of one hundred, the top position on the pyramid goes to . . ." The students were all sitting on the edge of their seats, and as I looked down at the paper, my eyes grew big and I took in a deep breath before I exclaimed, "Mr. Melvin Adams!" The look on his face was priceless. I could have just handed back the papers in a normal fashion, but doing it that way, drawing attention to his achievements, probably meant more to him than I will ever know.

As teachers and parents we have the freedom to lift up children and make them feel special. We can build confidence and self-esteem simply by taking the time to applaud good work and to show students how talented they are.

For years parents have been placing test papers and drawings on the refrigerator for everyone to see. I can remember my mom placing my papers on our old green refrigerator with this huge magnet that said, "I was Country when Country wasn't Cool." When I visit my sister's house, she has my nephew's work posted all over the kitchen. Displaying the work not only shows children that we love them and that we are proud of them, but it also builds their confidence and encourages them to produce more work that their parents can post as well.

The same theory applies in the classroom. Students need to see their work in the hall, on the door, on bulletin boards, and all over the classroom. Their achievements need to be showcased and highlighted wherever possible.

At Snowden Elementary we had a wonderful reading program called Reading Renaissance. Students would read books and then take tests on the computer. The program gave me printouts and let me know each student's reading ability and the level of books he or she should be reading. I could also get a printout that showed the amount of "reading points" each student had accumulated. Books of a higher level, which were longer, were worth more points than the shorter books of a lower reading level; therefore, the students who were reading shorter books had to read many more of them to equal the point total of the students who were reading at a more advanced level. Essentially, it all balanced out and was a very fair program. Getting my students to apply themselves, however, was a different story. I came up with a strategy to motivate the students to read more. During recess I took three pictures of every child. I let them pick the location. Some wanted to be on the swings, others on the monkey bars; some wanted to be holding a basketball or standing beside a tree. I wanted them to select the location because I needed this to be a picture they would like and want others to see, and I took three pictures of each student because I didn't want to take the chance of any of the kids having their eyes closed or with an embarrassing expression.

On my classroom door I placed the title, "Top Readers in the Fifth Grade," and I pasted ten pieces of blue construction paper from the top to the bottom of the door. Each week after I obtained the printout of the top readers, I would paste their pictures on the construction paper. (When the week was over, the pictures would peel right off. You have got to love the glue stick.)

As always I would make a big production of the top ten readers, and when I placed the pictures on the board, the students were about to burst with anticipation. Everyone who walked down the hall saw those pictures. Any parent who visited saw those pictures. The principal saw those pictures. Everyone saw those pictures, and the kids loved it. Some students who weren't reading on grade level would be on the door because they had really pushed themselves and read enough books to catch up with the advanced readers. There was always a mixture of levels on the door, and the pictures truly showed those who had applied themselves and deserved the distinction of a "Top Reader" for that week.

For those students who weren't on level, it did a world of good for their confidence. It was an honor for them to be on the door, and it inspired them to feel better about their reading abilities and to want to read more.

I visited a school where the principal had a similar idea in place. On the hallway beside his office was a sign, "Mr. Simpson's Stars," and below were about thirty stars of all different colors and sizes. In each one he had written a note telling about a certain student's accomplishment. One star said something like "Congratulations, James Branson!! I heard you have really been working hard in math class. I am very proud of you. Keep up the great work!" Some of the stars had test papers or other examples of work attached to them.

I asked Mr. Simpson how he knew what to write on each star, and he told me that he writes some of them because of things he has noticed throughout the school but that he gets the majority of the information from teachers who put test papers and notes in his box about students who are doing good work. He said that about every two weeks he pulls down the stars and delivers them to the students. The students can then take the stars home to show their parents.

There are many other ways to build confidence in students that don't involve displaying work or achievements. The best way, in my opinion, is just by telling students how much ability you see in them. I remember that when I was in tenth grade my typing teacher, Mrs. O'Neal, would always say to me when I walked in "Well, if it isn't the fastest typist in all of North Carolina." I don't even think I was the fastest typist in that class, but it sure made me feel good to hear Mrs. O'Neal say it. It built up my confidence, and it made me want to try harder.

If a teacher tells a student something positive, it feels great, but there are other ways to encourage students that can be even more effective. For example, calling or sending a note to a parent to point out good work on the part of a child can mean much more than if you only praise the child. Also, getting other teachers to make comments to students can be extremely effective. I would often tell my co-teachers or the principal about improvements some of my students were making, and I would ask them to mention to the students that I had said something to them. When they saw one of the students in the hall, they might say, "Hey Alice, Mr. Clark was telling me how well you have been doing in math class. Keep up the good work." When a child knows that you think enough of her efforts to share them with other teachers, that makes that student feel special and raises her confidence a great deal.

As a final word I would like to say that nothing raises the level of confidence in a child more than success. I know a high school math teacher who usually fails a great number of her classes. Most of the students fall into the C or D range, and they all talk about how much they dislike the teacher. I can tell she is trying to earn the students' respect by being tough, but she isn't doing a good job of teaching the material and is really lowering their confidence by failing those who normally perform extremely well in their classes.

Many teachers want to be strict and set the bar high for the students, but that isn't fair if the teachers are doing nothing to light a fire under the students and ensure that all of them have the information and skills needed to reach that bar and get over it.

8. HUMOR

*The most wasted of all days is
one without laughter.*

—E. E. CUMMINGS (1894–1962)

LAUGHTER IS UNIVERSAL. When we laugh we connect with each other in ways that help us relate, understand each other, and feel comfortable in any situation. When present in the learning environment, the joy and delight that come from humor can be powerful tools when getting students to put forth effort and achieve at the highest levels.

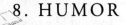 When It's Worth It Just to Laugh and Let It Go

I love a story my mother tells from her time in kindergarten. It was naptime and she was sitting right beside Bertha Moore, who she claims wore a bra and must have been four feet and one hundred pounds at the age of five.

Mom says that she was wide awake during naptime and that she noticed a chocolate candy bar with almonds in Bertha's desk. She says she can remember how hungry she was and how badly she wanted that candy bar and how it would just taste so good in her mouth. Finally Mom says she figured that Bertha didn't need it in the first place, and so she ate it.

Fifteen minutes later, Mom says that Bertha was crying, the teacher knew what had happened, and she was in big trouble. The teacher had sent for Mom's sister, my aunt Carolyn, from second grade to show her what her sister had done. Mom says she just kept denying over and over that she had eaten the candy bar, but she says that Carolyn turned beet-red when she saw the chocolate smeared all around Mom's mouth.

Mom says that she was scared to death to go home, and that her knees were knocking as Carolyn told their parents what Mom had done and how humiliated she was. My grandfather just looked at Mom and asked, "You were hungry, weren't you, sugar?" And that was the end of that.

When dealing with kids, it's a good idea to attempt to see things from their vantage point and find humor and understanding in their mistakes and embarrassing moments. It's all about putting things in perspective and realizing that minor frustrations and annoyances that can come from children aren't worth getting worked up over and making a mountain out of a molehill.

When I talk to my students, I try to help them deal with mistakes and embarrassing moments by showing them that it's okay to laugh at themselves. There are times in class where I have fallen down, knocked over a chalkboard, spilled cola all over my pants, and had many other embarrassing moments. When that happens, I just laugh, get up, and go about my business. One time I was teaching and a boy said, "Mr. Clark, you wore those same pants yesterday and you didn't wash them because that pen mark is still on the leg." I looked down and saw a brown smudge from the markers we were using the day before. It looked like a tree stump, and so I said, "What do you know? They sure are the same pants," and I took a green marker and added leaves to the top of the "tree." The kids all laughed, and I just smiled and moved on. If I had acted embarrassed, it would be sending the wrong message to the students. I remember when I was in elementary school my teacher came to school with two different shoes on. Everyone was afraid to point it out, and finally Stephen raised his hand and told her. She looked down, began to blush, and walked out of the room. We had an assistant watch us while the teacher went home to change shoes. I remember thinking how much fun it would have been if she had said she wore the shoes that way because she felt like being different. To a kid, being different can be really cool. If she had just said, "Oops," and laughed, then we all could have laughed and it would have been over.

It's always better just to laugh at those situations and

teach students not to be so uptight and to help them see the humor in mistakes and difficult situations.

✎ Understanding the Humor of Children

When I was coaching junior high basketball in North Carolina, there were several boys on the team who gave us problems. They were all around fourteen years old, and they were at that age where hormones are raging, no adult can relate, and disrespect comes naturally. The players were never disrespectful to me, but they were disrespectful to the other coach, Mr. Mitchell, and we were constantly torn about whether or not to leave the boys on the team because of their disrespect to him and the problems they were causing in their classes and around school. Normally, it would just be simple; they were disrespectful to other teachers and not performing well in school so they should be removed from the team. That was a tough call, though, because most of those boys lived to play basketball, and it was the main reason many of them were trying at all to keep their grades up and make an effort to behave. I was able to work with the team after school each day on their homework before we practiced, and without that structure most of them wouldn't have completed their assignments. If we kicked them off the team, they would be devastated and probably cause many more problems at school, but if we left them on the team we would be sending the wrong message to them and other students as well.

We were at an away game, and we had ridden there two hours on a cold bus because the heater was broken. It had just been a stressful day of teaching, and everything seemed to be going wrong. While the girls were playing, I was sitting with the boys, and, as always, I wouldn't let them slouch down and listen to their CD players. Listening to music was fine on the bus, but when the girls' game was going on I told them it was disrespectful. I asked them to sit up and watch as they played and root for them just as they would want to be cheered for themselves. Two boys, Tamiqus and Brandon, had run earpieces up through their shirts and stuck their CD players in their pants, thinking I wouldn't notice. After the girls' game, I took Tamiqus and Brandon into the locker room and told them how disappointed I was in them. They were both class clowns and had caused the most problems of any of the others on the team. They were constantly in trouble with Coach Mitchell, but I actually got along very well with them and I had stuck my neck out for them several times to keep them on the team. As I sat there telling them how upset I was with them they started to giggle. It was like they couldn't help it. They would just look at each other and then have to stifle laughter with all of their might. I couldn't believe how they were disrespecting me. Even when I threatened that they wouldn't play, they continued to giggle. Even when I asked if they wanted to be removed from the team, the laughter continued. Finally I said, "Okay, you're both off the team."

It just came out. I couldn't let them show disrespect in

their classes, to Coach Mitchell, and finally to me, after I had spent so much of my own time with the team at practices and games and after I had stuck up for them time and again. I had enough of the disrespect and I was fed up. Within five minutes, however, I regretted my decision, and I learned something very valuable. Whether you're a teacher or parent, it is never a good idea to make a decision when you are angry. Even when you feel certain that you are so sure of the punishment or what you want to say, calmer minds always see more with a clearer head, and taking the time to come to a decision will always lead to a better outcome. The second thing I learned is that sometimes teenagers don't have good control over their emotions. Sometimes they cry, sometimes they are angry, and sometimes they laugh. They are learning how to deal with these emotions, and sometimes because of their immaturity it is very difficult.

I can remember when I was in eighth grade and the math teacher gave us thirty minutes of free time in class so he could grade papers. My friend Monica and I decided to write letters to her cousin, whom I had met during the summer. We each wrote out entire letters, borrowed some envelopes, and addressed them. We then paid Pam Beavers for two stamps and placed them on the letters. I turned to Monica and handed her the letter I had written and said, "Will you mail this for me?" and she responded, "I'm not even going to mail this one."

When I think of that moment now, it doesn't seem

funny at all, but back in eighth grade I instantly started to howl and I slid out of my desk and onto the floor. It struck me funny and I just could not stop myself from laughing. Mr. File was standing over me asking if I was okay, but I could not even catch my breath to tell him I was fine. Even though I could tell he was angry, I couldn't manage to compose myself. As an adult, I can't remember the emotion that left me so helpless, but it was genuine back then.

Should I have kicked Tamiqus and Brandon off the team? I'm not sure. I do wish I had waited until I calmed down before I made such a quick judgment, and wish I had talked with them one on one instead of having them sit together. Giggling is contagious, and they were feeding off each other. The boys probably didn't deserve to remain on the team, but my heart is always pulled toward giving kids the opportunity to succeed, even when they seem to be dead-set against it.

Teenagers are a challenging group to understand, and it takes a special individual to work in a junior high school. When dealing with them, we need to be reminded of what we were like at their age, and how strong the emotions can be, and how the view of the world is completely different from fourteen-year-old eyes.

Appropriate Humor

I guess this one has always been a bit tricky for me. I love to laugh, and I think I always try to use humor to handle all different types of situations. Sometimes, however, it doesn't work. In fifth grade I can remember my teacher, Mrs. Edwards, who was extremely serious at all times. She hardly ever laughed, and one time when she was telling the class tons of information we were going to have to learn, I was just overwhelmed. I sat in the front row and threw up my hands and said a slogan from a very popular commercial at the time, "Calgon take me away!" Mrs. Edwards froze and paused for a few seconds. Silence filled the room and finally she said, "Well, Ron, if your ideal destination to be 'taken away' to is the office, then you have just gotten your wish." I was mortified.

When I was sixteen I was washing dishes at the local restaurant, The Legend. I was putting away the pots and I saw the owner, Mrs. Brenda, trying to get a huge vat of Thousand Island Dressing off the top shelf. She was on her tiptoes with her hands reaching as far up as they would go, inching the container slowly toward the edge. I could see it was about to fall, and I started rushing over to help. Unfortunately, I was too late and the entire vat tipped over and forty quarts of salad dressing covered Mrs. Brenda from head to toe. She immediately fell to the floor, forming one vast mound of orange dressing, and started howling with laughter. It was the funniest thing I had ever seen in my life, and I ran over and fell on the floor beside her, laughing along with her and holding my sides in pain. We were right in each other's faces just screaming with laughter, and then after about thirty seconds I realized something. Mrs. Brenda wasn't laughing, she was crying. Somehow I managed to keep my job.

When I started teaching, I was trying to find ways to relate to my students and get them to like being in my class. I attempted to use humor whenever possible, but one time I went too far and ended up hurting students in the process. For weeks the class had been talking about how two students, James and Heather, were boyfriend and girlfriend, but both of the students were shy, and I never saw them talk to each other or even act like they liked each other. I was putting up sentences on the board and asking the students to find the mistakes, and to try to add some spark to the assignment I decided to use some of the students' names. In the sentence I wrote:

this weekend james and his girlfriend

Here I paused and the class started mumbling and giggling, and I finished:

heather went to the american history museum

The class was roaring with laughter, and I looked out at James and Heather and saw they were red as radishes in the midday sun. I felt terrible. They both had their heads down, and I said to the class, "All right, that's enough," and I erased the sentence and put a new one in its place. The damage, however, was already done. I had not only embarrassed James and Heather, but they were also probably mad at me and I was sure I had lost some respect in their eyes. I learned never to use humor that could humiliate or make my students feel uncomfortable in any way.

Sometimes teachers will pick on students or call them nicknames and the students will laugh and go along with the joke as if it doesn't bother them. Usually this is because they don't know any other way to handle the situation, but in reality they are very uncomfortable. One of my former students who is now in high school has a teacher who calls him "Lil' bit." We were on a field trip and the other students were calling him that as well. He didn't seem to mind, but when I was talking to him later I asked him if it bothered him. He said, "Yes, and I wish they wouldn't call me that, but that's what the teacher calls me and there's nothing I can do about it." I know there are situations like that in every school where teachers are using nicknames or joking with students, and they don't realize that it really bothers the students. The children never say anything about it, and so the teachers feel they are okay with it. What makes it worse is that other students will follow the teachers' lead and they will start to carry on the joke as well.

It is important to be able to joke with students and have fun, but at the same time teachers need to make sure that the type of humor they are using isn't hurting or embarrassing any of the students.

✏ Trust Me on This One

Good teachers are always trying to find ways to spice up lessons and keep the learning process enjoyable and entertaining. When I was doing my student teaching with eleventh graders, I put together a big packet of review material on the Revolutionary War. As a cover sheet, I had a picture of George Washington upon his horse. At the last minute, I cut out a picture of my face and placed it on his body. When I passed out the packets, the kids doubled over laughing. They thought it was hilarious.

I decided to see what would happen if I put some of the kids' faces on different pictures for worksheets and tests. Using their yearbook photos, I started putting the students on the bodies of soldiers, scientists, athletes, and whoever had something to do with the material we were covering at the time. The kids absolutely loved it, and most of them were begging me to use their pictures next time.

When I started teaching fifth grade, I used the same strategy, but first I sent parents a letter asking for their permission to use their child's picture in the classroom for educational purposes. I then took a picture of each child and placed them in one folder. In another folder, I put old magazines and clippings I had gathered that might be good material. When I did a math worksheet, I left some room to the right for a picture. I'd then select a student, usually someone who needed a little push, and match up the face with something the kid liked. For example, if a student was a huge Lakers fan, I would put his face on Shaquille O'Neal. If the student wanted to become an astronaut, I would put her in a space suit. I was surprised at how realistic the pictures were, and the students were as well. Many would ask me, "Is that really me riding that horse?" or "Mr. Clark, when was I in that space suit?"

I found that the students whose pictures were on the worksheets worked harder and made sure to complete the work. They would often take it home and show it to their parents, which helped out on a number of different levels. It got to a point that at the end of the day, when I was about to pass out the homework worksheets, the students would all sit on the edge of their seats in anticipation. On days with no worksheets, they were disappointed. That was definitely a good sign.

For anyone willing to try this, I recommend that you first use your own picture. Test out the waters and see how your students react. They will probably all burst out laughing and think it's a hoot. Make sure you laugh along with them and let them know you think it's funny as well. If you decide to use the kids' pictures, set up two folders the way I did. This will save a lot of time and energy. Adding a picture to a worksheet usually takes me about 10 minutes of cutting and pasting, but it is well worth it when you see the students' reaction. Trust me on this one; it may seem different and it does take extra time, but you will definitely get a major reaction out of your students and it will add some excitement and humor to the day.

Using Humor to Relieve Stress

Laughing has a way of making us all feel better, and we tend to want to be around those who make us smile and enjoy

ourselves. Having a good laugh can also relieve a great deal
of stress. One year when we were about to take our end-of-
grade tests Mrs. Jones and I decided to have "Saturday
School." We wanted to give the students some extra review
before their tests on Monday and Tuesday, but we also
wanted to find a way to help them let off some steam, feel
good about themselves, and laugh.

The principal, Mrs. Roberson, opened the school for us,
and all of the students showed up. We reviewed hard for the
tests until noon, and then we told the students we had a surprise for all of their hard work. We took them to the library
where we had laid out pillows and cushions and we had
popcorn, drinks, and all kinds of snacks. We played games,
watched a funny movie, and just laughed and had a good
time. The students were so focused on the test and all bun-
dled up in knots, and Mrs. Jones and I just wanted to have
some time to allow them to kick back, relax, and have
some fun.

The University of North Carolina Tar Heels basketball team suffered a heartbreaking loss against its rival and
had to turn around two days later and play another
ranked team. The morale was extremely low, and I read
that Coach Williams did something unusual. To prepare
for the big game, instead of having a regular practice, he
had the starters coach the other players in a game. He said
he just wanted to lift their spirits and get them smiling
again. The players said they had a blast and enjoyed

cheering on their teams, relaxing, and laughing with each other.

Laughter is powerful. It can take away the blues, mend a heart, dry an eye, and doctor the soul. It can pull us together, lift us up, and put a smile on any face. In every classroom there should be some form of laughter. If the students are sitting through an entire lesson and no one laughs or smiles, then that classroom is missing something. Teachers should find a way to use their personalities to bring humor, laughter, and positive energy into their lessons whenever possible in order to make the students feel energized and cheerful and to make them enjoy being in the learning environment.

9. COMMON SENSE

*The freethinking of one age is
the common sense of the next.*

—MATTHEW ARNOLD (1822–1888)

WHEN I FIRST STARTED TALKING about my 55 Rules for my students, some people said they thought giving so many rules to students was ridiculous. What I found, however, is that when we are more specific with children and let them know exactly what we expect from them, they are far more willing to try to live up to those expectations. I am afraid that sometimes we just tell students to be more organized or to behave, not realizing that sometimes what we see as common sense isn't so clear to children. Teachers and parents need not only to have common sense but to take the time with children to develop skills with them that others see as obvious.

✐Using Common Sense When Dealing with Children

The number one thing parents and teachers can do to positively affect the lives of our children and students is to become more aware of the way we speak to them. That seems obvious to me, but in my experiences of dealing with parents and other teachers, it seems that many don't realize how powerful our words can be. Children see themselves reflected in our eyes, and if we are constantly saying things like "You never do your homework" or "You are so disrespectful" or "You are always rude," they will begin to believe it. They start to feel that they are disrespectful and rude, that those negative connotations are part of who they are. Over time, being so negative with children can really take its toll. I will never forget the parents of one of my students who always came to conferences with their youngest child. I always said something like "She is such a sweet little girl," and her mom would inevitably respond, "No, she ain't. She bad." I would turn to the little girl and say, "Tamatha, you aren't bad, are you?" and the little girl would twist her hair, look up, and say, "I'm baaad." After hearing that all the time, I am sure she began to believe she really was bad.

What I have learned this year from the schools and communities I have visited is that when parents and teachers make a conscious effort to lift up children, to support them, to praise them, and to acknowledge their successes, those students will have pride in themselves and far more confidence, and their grades will be much higher. There is a school in Phoenix, Arizona, that is really doing it right. All the faculty members have been instructed to make every attempt to be positive with all the children. They are never supposed to be negative or focus on weaknesses or belittle children. The entire atmosphere at the school is focused on supporting those kids and lifting them up, and it is obvious from the moment you walk in the door. I was greeted by a group of students who gave me a guided tour of the school. They introduced me to all the faculty members and to many of their classmates. They were so proud of their school, excited about learning, and respectful. As I walked down the halls, their work filled the walls in colorful displays of their accomplishments. Believe it or not, some elementary schools I visited didn't even post students' work in the hallways. This school, however, was overflowing with pride, support, and love.

People often ask about my parents and how they raised me. I think the most wonderful thing about my parents is that they never once said anything negative about me or my ideas. They were always loving and supportive, and they never said anything to make me feel bad about myself. There were times when they had to be stern and punish me, but they never saw the need to raise their voices or scold me in a way that would belittle me.

How we talk to our children and our students is crucial. We have to support them, make them feel good about themselves, and tell them things that focus on their talents, their abilities, and their potential.

Commonsense Ways to Help Children Become Organized

Every year it always baffles me how disorganized students can be. It can take up to ten minutes for a child to find all his homework, and when it does appear, it often contains smears, wrinkles, and soup stains. I could never understand why it was so hard to be organized, and then I realized that in most cases no one had ever taken the time to actually show the students how to structure all their material and keep it in order. One summer I went out and bought a set of the supplies I was going to expect my students to purchase for the year. I took them home, laid them out on the floor, and took a picture of them. I then sent the students a letter along with the picture of the supplies and a description of each item. I know this may seem as if I was overdoing it a bit, but I was tired of having students walk in on the first day of school with supplies they didn't need. I always had to send the parents back out to buy additional notebooks and other materials, and it usually took weeks before my students had what they needed. Also, during the weeks before school, the number one question asked by parents is "What school supplies does my child need?" I decided to be proactive and answer that question before it reached me.

When my students enter the classroom with all their material, I go through the items and tell them what each one will be used for. They label the notebooks with their name and the subject, and I ask them to make sure they use that notebook only for work in that subject. In all, ten components make up each binder:

1. Five notebooks—one for each subject, plus an extra one. The extra notebook is used for writing letters or notes to other students, drawing, and scrap paper. If you don't include that notebook, the students will use paper from their subject notebooks, and it will become less organized. (All notebooks fit into the three-ring binder. I ask my students to get the 2½-inch binder to make sure all the material will fit.)

2. Homework folder—where the students keep all uncompleted homework. I make sure that as the homework worksheets are being passed out to the class, each student places the assignment in this folder.

3. Graded folders—used for graded work. They must have two. One is marked "Homework,"

and the other "Tests." It can be a struggle to get the students to keep failing papers, but I tell them I will give five extra points to any failing test paper that is in the binder during a parent-teacher conference. I then remind them that I know what they make on each test, and if a paper is missing, I will tell their parents what the score was and also inform them that five extra points were missed because the student removed the test.

4. Homework notebook—where the students enter their daily homework assignments. It is so important, especially for elementary and middle school students, that the teacher take the time to make sure the homework is being copied down correctly by each student. It also helps to have this notebook because my parents know exactly where to look to see what the assignments are for the night. They also know to look in Folder A to find any homework worksheets.

When the students copy down each assignment, I ask them to place a box beside each task. When they have completed it, I tell them to draw an X in the box. This is a way of getting the students to double-check that they have completed all the assignments.

5. Personal journal—which students use at least three times a week. I grade the journal on Thursdays, and I give the students five minutes in class to complete their entry. This is done before the bell rings, and I ask the students to leave their journal on the correct page and just place it facedown on their desks. I then walk around the room and check to see that the students have made good entries. Basically, I tell them they can write about anything they want as long as it expresses emotion and/or falls into one of the following categories:

> Tell how you feel about a certain topic.
> Write about something that happened to you recently.
> Describe something you are looking forward to.
> Tell something you have learned.
> Explain what happened in your most recent dream.
> Write about something you enjoy.

I find that giving the students those prompts gets greater results than just saying, "Write about your day," or "Write anything you want."

I usually don't read each student's entire entry. I quickly place a letter grade on the page, occasionally make a brief comment or two, and then I move on. I try not to spend too much time on the journals because the point is to make sure the students are expressing themselves, not that they are being grammatically correct or using perfect structure. I wouldn't want to stifle their creativity in their journals by filling them with red "teacher marks."

As always with writing assignments, I share examples of my own writing with my students. I keep my own journal and make overheads of my entries to show the class.

6. Loose-leaf paper—which is needed when assignments must be turned in to avoid having those perforated edges everywhere.

7. A ruler, calculator, pens, pencils, crayons, and calendar. I recommend that my students get a ruler that has three holes so that it can be attached in the binder. The calculator, pens, pencils, and crayons are placed in a slot in the front of the binder. If the binder does not come with a slot for those items, clear plastic folders with zippers can be purchased that work perfectly.

I give my students two calendars that I photocopy, laminate, and punch holes in. The first calendar shows the days we are in school, and the second one contains the lunch menu and changes each month.

8. A folder for graded papers—which is where all graded material is placed.

9. Flash card holders. We make a lot of flash cards in my class, and I want the students to have a place to keep them so that they don't get lost or end up scattered all over our classroom floor. We use the clear plastic pocket folders that fit right into the binder. I pass out those really thick rubber bands and have the students keep extras in the folder so that they never run out. If you hand out the really thin rubber bands, at recess the students might have a battle royal with them, so it is better to use the thick ones. They are harder to pop, and they don't stretch as much. I've never had any problems with them.

10. My 55 Essentials—is handed out. I give the class rules to the students and have them include the list in their binder. It is always good to have a list of the guidelines, procedures, and consequences handy.

Each day before the students leave I also mention to them exactly what books they will need that night. For some reason there are kids who feel they have to take home every book every night, and they will walk out of my classroom looking like struggling turtles just trying to put one foot in front of the other. To keep this from happening, I tell them to take only the necessary material, and I point out each day what that is.

On the first day of school I go through each item on the list with my students and show them where to place each of them in the binder. For the first couple of weeks I take the time to help them copy down their homework, place items in the correct folders, and keep their work in the appropriate notebook. It can take about ten minutes at the end of class just to get the homework assignments delivered. As the year goes on, however, the students get the hang of the system, and by the end of the year it is a quick and efficient process. The main reason for all this effort in getting kids organized is that they will use those skills during the school year and also will continue to be organized in the future. It always makes me feel so good to hear teachers in high school say how organized and efficient my former students are. It is something that seems simple and commonsensical, but the idea of being organized is foreign to a lot of kids, and they need someone—a teacher, parent, or friend—to give them guidance and show them how they can become more efficient.

✏ Commonsense Ways to Keep New Teachers from Leaving the Profession

Entering the profession can be quite challenging, and it is a shame to see so many exceptional teachers leave the profession after teaching only a few years. They enter with so much energy and zest, but they soon burn out. I was fortunate that a wonderful veteran teacher took me under her wing and taught me the essential tricks of the trade that you don't learn in college: how to work the copy machine, the secretary's favorite candy, how to deal with parents and other teachers, filling out field trip forms, what to do if the children vomit. Most new teachers are thrown in without life support. How can we keep that from happening and keep new teachers in the profession?

A. Parents of students with first-year teachers should do whatever they can to support them. Volunteer for field trips and to help out in the classroom. If there is a problem, take it easy on the teacher. State your concern but remember that he or she is going through a learning process. If you don't feel that the teacher is teaching your child adequately, do what you can at home to supplement the curriculum. Take an active role and make sure you know what is going on in the classroom. Make every effort to give the teacher a chance and to

discuss your concerns with the teacher before
going to the administration.

B. First-year teachers should *not* be given the most
challenging classes. I have seen all across the country how first-year teachers get the shaft in terms of
receiving the students who have the most difficult
disciplinary problems. Some veteran teachers feel
that they have earned the right to select their students, and they are given a voice in their schools to
make that decision. It is a detriment to the system
when such educators take the easier road at the
expense of new teachers. Administrators who make
out class lists need to be aware of the students in
each grade to the point where class assignments can
be developed with concern for first-year teachers. If
a computer is assigned to select the class lists, that
method needs to be reconsidered.

C. In most schools, mentor teachers are assigned to
new teachers. In some cases those mentors don't
offer the proper guidance. All veteran teachers
should make an effort to welcome new teachers
and make them feel at home. Learn their names.
Place notes of encouragement on their desks.
Share lesson plans and supplies. Help them with
their bulletin boards. Make them lunch. Show

them everything they need to know to fit in and have a chance to be successful. Be a friend and, most important, be positive.

D. Do not place first-year teachers on every committee in the school. The first year is hard enough without having to sit through endless meetings and be responsible for countless extracurricular duties. Spare them. Let them be in their classrooms. When I asked as many first-year teachers as I could what was the main problem they faced as a teacher, the most common response was "Time." That in my opinion is the answer of an exceptional educator, one who never has enough time to do all he or she wants to do for the students. However, that is also the answer of teachers who are going to burn out quickly if we overload them. When they are first getting their feet wet, let new teachers focus on the main reasons they are there: to teach their students with passion, to devote ample time to their lessons, and to enjoy the experience of being a teacher.

✏ Using Common Sense Leads to Better Results

When I first started teaching, there were times when I poured all my heart and effort into my lessons, and then I would test my students and they would do poorly. I couldn't understand what I was doing wrong. I would stress over and over how important it was for them to study, and they, along with their parents, would all assure me that the kids had studied. Then one day a young girl said, "Mr. Clark, you are going to be so proud of me. To prepare for the test I copied the whole chapter," and she showed me that she had actually copied the entire chapter, word for word, out of the book. I realized then that even if those kids were spending hours studying, many of them probably weren't using their time wisely.

I started taking time each year to show kids how to study. I gave them my Ten Tips for Tackling Tests, and I took the time to discuss each one with the students and show them exactly what each tip meant and how it could help them better prepare for their tests. Here are the Ten Tips for Tackling Tests:

1. *Make flash cards.* I showed them how to make flash cards. I told them to put a vocabulary word on one side and the definition on the other. I told them to hold them in their hands, to look at the word, and to try to say the definition. Then I told them to check to see if they were correct. Now that seems like the most obvious thing in the world to me, but those students weren't doing it.

Another big plus about having flash cards is that once they are made, kids can go to parents, siblings, or friends and get them to give a pop test. All they have to do is read the definition and see if the student is able to say the correct vocabulary word or answer to the question. Also, I encourage the students to write key questions on the cards and put the answers on the back. This will enable the study partner to really test to see that the information has been learned even if the study partner has no prior knowledge of the topic.

2. *Read the summaries of each chapter.* Sometimes when we had unit tests, the students would say they felt as if they should read the entire unit again, and they would begin at chapter 1, but they wouldn't finish, usually not even getting halfway. What I found was that those students weren't really paying attention to what they were reading. They were just doing what I call "eye reading," where they are looking at the words but not really thinking about what is being said. By having the students just review the summaries and really pay attention to what is being said, they are more likely to obtain the key bits of information they need to know for the test.

3. *Pay close attention to photographs, diagrams, and captions.* Most students don't realize the importance of anything that isn't in the text, but I tell them that very often key questions on their tests come from information they were supposed to learn from looking at diagrams, graphs, charts, and pictures located within their books. I used that technique myself a lot in college. The first thing I did to prepare for any test was look at the photographs and captions. As I tell my students, if the picture was important enough to be placed in the book, then it usually has an important purpose and there is something the author wants you to learn or realize by looking at the photograph.

4. *Take note of anything written in bold letters.* I tell my students to go through the text and pay close attention to all words in bold. I point out that these are usually key vocabulary words, and I suggest that they read the sentence before and after the word to make sure they have a good understanding of the meaning.

5. *Read over the notes from class.* This also requires teaching the students how to take notes. If you go to any class in America and ask the students to take notes, there will be many students who will

assume they need to write down everything that the teacher says. Every year I would have kids working frantically and asking me to slow down. In the end, those notes were not even legible, and they were essentially useless. I finally told my kids that when I ask them to take notes, I want them to look for the "three s's." They should take note of something if I

slow down when I say it. This is a big clue to them that I am giving time to write it down.

stress it over and over. If I tend to repeat something, it is probably important. If they have already written it, I tell them that the second and third time I say it, they should just underline it. That way when they are reviewing their notes, they will remember it was important.

stop to write it on the board, especially if it is a diagram or chart.

Another thing I tell my students is that when they hear information in the classroom, they are probably thinking they won't forget it. Sometimes I have instructed kids to take notes and they have told me they know they will remember the information. That is a big mistake because usually a lot of information is covered, and often dates, times, and information get confused. Reminding the kids to write down information, even when they feel they won't forget it, is a good idea. I tell my students I not only want them to remember the information for the test, but I want them to remember it for as long as possible, and writing it down and reviewing it will greatly help.

6. *Review all pop quizzes and chapter tests.* Some subjects, especially math, usually have wonderful chapter tests with the answers in the back of the book. I encourage my students to take the tests and then check to see how they did. For the ones they missed I tell them to try to work out the problem until they are able to see how the correct answer was determined. For pop quizzes I tell them that they can make their own tests. All they have to do is copy down the questions on another sheet of paper and attempt to answer them. When they are finished, they can check the original pop test to see how they did.

7. *Study with a friend.* I tell my students that it is always a good idea to study with a partner because

many times classmates may have copied down important notes that others might have missed. It's always good to see another student's perspective when it comes to copying down lecture comments.

8. *Make sure you have a morning review.* Sometimes students can study two or three hours at night, but then when they wake up, some of the information has slipped away. It is always a good idea to have note cards at the breakfast table, on the bus, in the carpool, and while waiting for the school bell to ring. Students shouldn't assume because they studied the night before that they are prepared. It is best to make sure to refresh the mind with all that has been learned as close to the actual test time as possible.

9. *Get a good night's rest.* Nothing bothers me more than seeing a student falling asleep during a test or hearing a stomach growling. I know that child is not able to perform to the best of his abilities. I tell my students that when they take a test, they need to be physically as well as mentally prepared. Doing commonsense things like getting a good night's sleep and eating a balanced breakfast are

essential to performing well. I can remember
when I was in high school and I went to take the
SAT. I was late for the test, and when I arrived, I
couldn't find my admissions ticket. I was looking
all over the place and frantic. I ended up running
in at the last minute, my heart racing. That is not
the type of emotional state kids should be in
when taking tests. I ask my students' parents to be
mindful of test dates and to make sure that their
kids arrive on time and prepared with all the
necessary materials.

10. *Don't be afraid to ask for help.* This is a mistake
many students make, whether they are in
elementary school, high school, or college. It
never hurts to ask the teacher or professor for
extra help. Many teachers will provide their notes,
the use of their overhead sheets, and advice on
what to concentrate on for the test, or they will
offer other helpful tips that will lead students in
the right direction. At the very least asking for
help will show the teacher that the student really
cares about the test, and that he wants to do well
and perform to the best of his abilities. As a
teacher I appreciate when students ask for extra
help. I usually tell them what they need to focus
on or give them a hint or two on what the essay

question might be. I am always more than willing to do that but only if the students ask during recess, lunch, or after class. The mistake some students make is that they ask during class in front of the other students. When trying to get individual help, this is not the time to do it.

✑ Common Sense Saves Time

Taking the time to show students how to take notes, study, review information, and be organized can save them a great deal of time. It can also make life a lot easier for parents and teachers. When students have the skills to learn, prepare for tests, and organize their materials on their own, it saves a lot of effort that usually falls on the shoulders of others. It also makes it easier for teachers when they are reviewing schoolwork with parents. Whenever I have parent meetings, I simply pull out each student's binder and show it to the parents. In each section, whether it is math, writing, or another subject, all I have to do is flip through the section and point out various strengths and weaknesses. One key area that always stands out is writing. As we flip the pages, we can see the progression in writing and how much improvement has been made. When the parents question why their children scored a certain grade, I can turn to the "Tests" section and pull out their old tests. It makes life much easier.

During my time in New York City, the nicest thing the principal said to me was when she walked in my room on parent-teacher night. I had a welcome sign-in table and a refreshment table with drinks, cookies, and pizza. She looked at me and said in a disgusted tone, "Oh, Mr. Clark. Have you reduced yourself to bribing the parents?" I thought I had done such a good job, and I was so upset. I explained to her that many of the parents had negative feelings about school and most of them never come for parent-teacher conferences because they are tired of hearing negative reports on their kids. I then told her how I was willing to do whatever it took to get them in that classroom and involved with their child's learning process. The principal just grimaced as she walked over to a student's desk. Using one hand, she flipped open the binder that was sitting on the desk. As she turned page after page, her eyes got bigger and bigger. Thinking she probably had chosen the best student's desk, she moved down a row and to the side, selecting another binder and again flipping it open with one hand. Then, down the row and across two aisles, she opened another. Finally she said, "Mr. Clark, this is amazing. How have you gotten these students to perform at this level?" I had spent hours talking with her in her office, trying to get her to see how my teaching strategies were working, and then in the span of one minute and with the help of the binder all her doubts had been erased, and the weight of the world was off my shoulders.

I would recommend that all teachers and parents take the time to help students learn to be self-sufficient when it comes to their schoolwork. In doing so they will become more organized and more efficient, and a great deal of time will be saved.

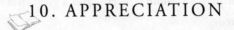10. APPRECIATION

As we express our gratitude, we must never forget that the highest appreciation is not to utter words, but to live by them.

—JOHN F. KENNEDY (1917–1963)

I T IS IMPORTANT FOR US as teachers to show appreciation and also to get our students to understand the importance of being appreciative. Even more important, however, I believe that as teachers we should feel a great deal of gratitude for the opportunity we are given to work with our students. Every day parents place their trust in us that we are going to guide, support, and educate their children in a way that lifts them up and helps them become better people. That is a big responsibility, and we should not take it lightly. We should approach teaching as a gift, a privilege, and an occupation that we are honored to have.

The Importance of Showing Appreciation

I always stress to my students that as they go through life it is important to show gratitude to those who help them along the way. I tell them that if someone sees that you really appreciate what they have done for you, more likely they will want to help you again in the future.

Using that philosophy is one of the main ways I am able to get so much funding for class projects and trips. When I first approach businesses about making contributions to my class, they are usually willing to give only a very small amount. Even if it is only ten dollars, I have all my students write thank-you cards and letters. I then give the principal, and sometimes the superintendent, a list of the businesses that have contributed money, and I ask them to send a short note of thanks. Later, when I call the businesses, they say they were overwhelmed by all the wonderful cards and letters they received and that they are embarrassed they gave only a small amount. I just respond, "That's okay. Actually, we are starting another project now and would love to have your help."

Using gratitude in that way helps develop a wonderful partnership between many businesses and my classroom. What I have found is that there is money out there and people are willing to contribute, but the key is that they want to know where the money is going, how it is going to be used, and that their efforts will be appreciated.

There are many other times when showing appreciation can really make an impact. My friend Michelle is a professional at giving interviews. She has never applied for a job that she hasn't gotten, and I was talking to her about her techniques. She told me that she always sends thank-you cards to the members of the interview committee. She said that in the card she thanks them for their time and lets them know how much she appreciated the opportunity to talk with them about the exciting and challenging position. Michelle told me that when her current boss called to tell her she had received the job, he made a point of telling her how impressive her card was. He said that the committee already liked her, but after getting the cards, they knew without a doubt that her attention to detail and thoughtfulness made her just the type of person they wanted working in their corporation.

My friend Bith always talks about how there are "good dinner guests" and "bad dinner guests." She says good guests will never show up empty-handed. They always have a dessert, flowers, wine, or some other item to show gratitude. As soon as the meal begins, she says, good guests will immediately make a comment about the quality of the food. Bith says she is always nervous that they won't like what she has prepared, and the longer she has to sit there without their telling her they are enjoying the meal, the more anxious she becomes. The best guests, Bith adds, will even say they enjoy something so much that they would like to have the recipe.

Bith says she invites her good guests over all the time. She says she enjoys their company and the fact that they understand all the time, work, and effort she put into making the meal and the night special. She still loves her bad dinner guests as friends, but she tends to meet them out for dinner instead of having them over to her home.

At school I talk with the students about how important it is to go out of your way to show appreciation to those who help you. I point out how the custodians are working hard every day to make the school the best possible environment for them to learn in. In order to thank them, I have the students bring in drinks, chips, and covered dishes from home, and at lunchtime we spread tablecloths on the desks, set out the food, turn down the lights, put on some soft music, and hang a banner that reads, "We appreciate you!" While we are at lunch, we ask the custodians to come to our room to enjoy the special meal prepared just for them. I cannot tell you how much it means to them that we would go out of our way to thank them for all they do. Surprisingly, I find that my trash cans are emptied more often, and on several occasions I have walked in to find that the night before my room had been swept, mopped, and cleaned. We weren't looking for any extra treatment for our room, but it was nice to see that the custodians also thought enough of what we did for them that they wanted to show us gratitude in return.

In so many forms, showing appreciation is not only a

kind and considerate thing to do but is a way of letting others know that we realize the time and energy they put in to help us and others. When people feel that others notice their efforts, they are much more likely to continue their hard work.

✏ Appreciation for Teachers

The key to improving education in America isn't more technology, newer schools, bigger libraries, higher test scores, or even lower class size. All those things play a part, but the factor that above all others has the greatest impact on our students is the classroom teacher. There are schools in America without technology and libraries, and students who have outdated books; still, their grades and test scores are very high. The main reason is that there are dedicated, intelligent, and enthusiastic teachers in those classrooms. So the question is, Why don't we have teachers like that in every classroom? I think one reason, unfortunately, is that teacher pay is not in proportion to the expectations of the job. People have said to me that traveling across the country giving speeches for an entire year must have been the hardest year of my life. Actually, it was nothing compared with one year in the classroom. As teachers we are drained each day mentally, physically, and emotionally, and there cannot be a harder job. One might argue that the job of a parent is far more challenging, and I won't argue that point, but, actually, good teachers, truly excellent teachers, view their students as if they were their own children, and during the school year they feel the pressure of making a life's worth of difference in each one of those students. It is a stressful and daunting task. I can remember growing up and thinking, "Being a teacher can't be that difficult. I mean, geez, they get the summers off." I could not have been more naive. It is incredibly difficult, and it is a shame teachers aren't compensated in a way that is equal to the amount of effort that is required.

When I was in college, I had several friends, most of them males, who were interested in becoming teachers, but they decided against it because they wanted to earn a good enough living to support a family. They didn't want to have to work a second job during the summer or live from paycheck to paycheck. As a teacher I have seen several of my colleagues quit and leave the profession because they were offered double the pay in other fields. When you are trying to raise a family, that type of money is tempting. But I am not saying that teachers are overly concerned with their pay. If they were, they probably wouldn't be teachers. However, if teacher salaries were more competitive with those in the business world, we would begin to recruit the best possible individuals out of college to join the profession. Soon all classrooms would have teachers who were motivated, intelligent, enthusiastic, and devoted to providing the students with the best possible education. Isn't that what we want?

What is the key to improving education in America?

Giving teachers adequate compensation and recruiting the best possible individuals out of college to become the teachers of the next generation is a great start. In addition, something that everyone can do is treat teachers with respect and show them how much we appreciate what they do.

✎ How Can Administrators Show Appreciation for Teachers?

No other individual has more impact on the school environment than the principal. He or she sets the tone for the year, serves as an example for the staff, and makes decisions that affect the entire faculty and all of the students. The best principals are the ones who have extremely high expectations with even higher levels of appreciation for hard work, dedication, and effort. They gain the trust and admiration of the staff, who are then more willing to listen to his or her ideas, to put forth more effort, and to try to reach the goals that have been set. In reality, the strength of a principal is measured by his or her ability to bring out the best attributes of the staff and get them to use their talents, intelligence, and creativity to meet the needs of all students.

In order to produce those types of results, it is crucial that administrators show gratitude. An appreciated staff will go to the moon for an effective administrator, while a stifled and belittled staff will spread negativity throughout the entire school.

Here are some ways administrators can show gratitude and help to create an environment where teachers and students feel that their efforts are noticed and appreciated.

• *Give unconditional support.* I often ask teachers to tell me one characteristic of a good principal, and the most frequent answer is that the best principal gives outstanding support where parents are concerned. This is an issue that is important as an educator, because parents can at times become upset, irrational, and unreasonable with teachers, even when dealing with minor things such as the amount of homework given or the number of times the class goes to the restroom in one day. It can be a horrible feeling to have parents show up at the classroom door to rake you across the coals; when put in a position where their abilities are questioned, teachers need to feel they are supported. At Snowden Elementary, my principal, Mrs. Roberson, was excellent when it came to dealing with parents, and I felt safe knowing that she would have my back. She told me one time, "Mr. Clark, I will always support my staff at all costs, unless someone breaks a rule that goes against school policy." It meant a lot to me that she was so confident in our abilities, and her trust in me and her willingness to take on the duty of dealing with parents led me to develop great respect for her.

Principals, don't play politics with parents and leave your staff hanging. Let them know you trust them, you support them, and that you have their backs.

• *Don't overload the plate.* There is a tendency by principals to place a lot of responsibility on the plate of teachers who are capable, dependable, and efficient. The problem is that those teachers may become overloaded. When one of my former administrators would ask me to perform extra duties, I had to say yes because if I didn't I was given a guilt trip. It is a hard thing for teachers to say no, but when they do, principals should respect that and not push the issue.

• *Ask for ideas.* My second year teaching, Mrs. Roberson called Mrs. Jones and me into the office. She said that she needed to talk with us about something important, and went on to tell us that she had been given a sum of money and she wanted our ideas on how to best reward the students for being an Exemplary School. She said that she trusted our judgment and wanted us to use the money in whatever way we felt appropriate. When we walked out of that office, Mrs. Jones and I were dancing down the hall. It was a great feeling that we were going to get to spend the money on the students, but it was an even better feeling that Mrs. Roberson appreciated us enough to get our ideas.

Principals are responsible for making decisions daily. When possible, they should take the time to ask for input from teachers, secretaries, custodians, and the entire staff. Sometimes sharing the decision-making process will go a long way to building respect and creating ownership in the school environment.

• *Be fair.* If any members of the staff are treated differently, trust me, the entire faculty will know about it. Teachers notice things like who gets the best schedule, who doesn't have to serve lunch duty, who leaves early and misses a faculty meeting, who has the best furniture, and who gets the most supplies. It is a difficult task for a principal to manage, because treating everyone exactly the same way is almost impossible. Administrators should, however, be aware that most teachers are aware of how others in the school are being treated, and that is something that can lead to dissension when favoritism is shown.

• *Be an example of your expectations.* Good principals should not harp on teachers about getting to school early if they themselves come to school late each day. Principals should not question when a teacher needs to take a personal day off if they do not have to report their reasons for taking leave. Principals should not demand enthusiasm and hard work when they are not putting all of their heart, effort, and soul into the school. One of the great keys to being a successful principal is to lead by example. If an administrator is committed, dedicated, and passionate about educating children, then that fire will usually spread throughout the entire faculty.

• *Have an open-door policy.* In the eyes of teachers, this one is major. It seems so simple, but teachers notice how often the principal's office door is open or closed. When it is open, the teachers feel free to walk in, knock on the door, or say a quick hello. When it is closed, it sends a message of isolation, foreboding, and inaccessibility.

• *Respect teachers' time.* This issue comes up most often when discussing teacher meetings. If there is going to be a faculty meeting, the principal must be there on time, there must be a good reason for the meeting, and the principal must not allow the session to drag on and on. Thirty minutes is a good amount of time for a faculty meeting after school.

• *Handle disciplinary matters immediately.* In my experiences, I have seen administrators who handled discipline problems quickly and effectively, and I have also seen some who let the issues linger for days before taking action on the matter. In some cases, I would see a teacher write up a student for being disrespectful and causing problems in the classroom. By the time the student was called to the office, which could be days later, the student was no longer a problem and was paying attention in class. By that time, removing the student from the class totally defeats the purpose. In order to be effective, discipline, like rewards, should be swift and appropriate. Good principals understand that, and they realize that if teachers get to a point where they have to write up a child and ask an administrator for help, then they need to respect and act on the matter quickly.

• *Give instant feedback after observations.* This can drive teachers insane. After a formal observation, teachers are very anxious to hear feedback. They have had to teach an entire lesson while an administrator watches in silence, and then *poof,* they're gone, without an encouraging word or any positive affirmation. In some schools I have visited, the teacher leaves with the principal immediately after the lesson, and a substitute takes over the class. The substitute is hired for the entire day, and she or he floats from class to class, filling in for fifteen minutes after each observation. This is an excellent solution for teachers, principals, and students.

After the lesson is discussed, the teacher returns to class and after school the administrator writes up the lesson more formally. That system works really well and takes a lot of pressure off the teachers. In some schools, however, it can be days and even weeks before the lesson is discussed. Many principals feel they need to type up the formal observation before meeting with the teacher, but that is wasting a lot of time that many teachers will spend stressed out and apprehensive as they await the outcome.

• *Learn the names of all students.* I once attended a sixth-grade graduation where the principal pronounced about a quarter of the names incorrectly. It was an embarrassment, and many of the parents in the audience gladly let her know how offended they were. Learning and remembering some-one's name is the most basic form of respect, and it amazes me how a principal can run a school without learning the identity of every single student.

• *Give freedom for creativity and new ideas.* The best teachers come up with creative ideas, strategies, and programs, and the best principals are willing to give them the chance to explore the new techniques. So many times, I would walk into Mrs. Roberson's office and smile, and she would say, "Whatever it is, NO," but then I would sit down and explain my idea. She would listen and almost always agreed to give me the freedom to try what I had in mind. I appreciate that confidence she had in me. She didn't always agree with me or think my strategies would work, but she was willing to let me try them anyway. That type of trust means a great deal to teachers, and the best principals are willing to empower their staff and allow them to attempt their new and different ideas.

✎ How Can Teachers Show Appreciation for Administrators?

An administrator's job is not an easy one, but it is made even more difficult without the support of the teachers. In some situations principals can be a thorn to get along with, and it takes a lot of the joy out of teaching. When that occurs, however, it is important that we remember our students and act in a way that will improve the school environment rather than destroy it. Here are some suggestions for handling those situations where we have questionable leadership. Keep in mind that these are also ways that we can show respect to those outstanding principals as well. The majority of administrators are phenomenal. They are passionate, driven, and dedicated, and they need our support and appreciation.

• *Avoid negativity.* Negativity breeds negativity. The school environment can be tense, but even when we feel anger toward the administration for giving us extra bus duty, putting us on another committee, or questioning our abilities, we have to avoid speaking negatively about the situation in front of our students or their parents. That is highly unprofessional, and sends a horrible message.

In addition, avoid being negative around first-year teachers. I remember hearing a new teacher say how she loved the principal and was so appreciative of being hired, and a veteran teacher said, "You just wait, she'll get her claws in you before too long." The poor girl's eyes bugged out of her head.

I have been there and I have worked under challenging administrations, but focusing on the negative to a new and enthusiastic teacher does absolutely nothing to improve the classroom or school environment.

• *Dress appropriately.* One issue that principals bring up often is how difficult it is to get teachers to dress in a professional manner. This totally blows my mind, because if we want to be treated like professionals we should dress like professionals. Also, when teachers are in a dress, pantsuit, or suit and tie, the students are much more respectful and disciplinary problems are minimized. Why so many teachers continue to wear sweatpants, jeans, and other inappropriate clothing to school escapes me. If we dress professionally it's a lot more likely that we'll be treated that way by the students, the parents, and the administration.

• *Handle discipline in the classroom.* There are circumstances where a student needs to be sent to the office and written up. There are other times, however, when teachers should attempt to handle the situation in the classroom or just outside the classroom door and relieve the administration of the burden of handling every situation that arises. If we want them to take our disciplinary concerns seriously, we can't turn to them with every problem that comes up.

• *Pay attention during meetings.* Teachers can be the world's worst when it comes to paying attention at meetings. It's almost as if we enjoy acting out the personalities of the worst students in our classes. Principals can see who is paying attention and who isn't, and during meetings a great way to show respect is to look the administrator in the eyes, stop grading the papers, avoid passing notes, and give your full attention.

• *Respect decisions.* Sometimes administrators make decisions that the faculty doesn't agree with. I learned early on that sometimes these choices are made with information that can't be shared with everyone, and instead of making a quick and negative judgment, it is a good idea to have faith that the administration has the best interests of the students at heart. Teachers sometimes don't know and shouldn't know all that goes on behind closed doors.

• *Cover the curriculum.* When I ask principals what one thing their teachers could do to make their lives easier, they almost always say, "Teach, and teach well." The best way to respect and help the administration is just to make sure the curriculum is being covered and that the students are enjoying learning and that they are achieving. Principals are much easier to get along with and they will be much more supportive if they know a teacher is doing an excellent job educating the students.

• *Be part of the solution.* When the students aren't motivated, there are weak teachers, or the school's test scores are low, it is always easy to place the blame on the administration. The best way to help the situation, however, is to ask yourself what you can do to make improvements and have a positive impact on the school. It might involve tutoring after school, sharing lesson plans with other teachers, or finding various ways to improve the school environment, but no matter what way teachers contribute, it's all about taking ownership for the condition of the school instead of placing the blame on others. As the saying goes, if you're not part of the solution, you're part of the problem.

How Parents Can Show Appreciation for Teachers

Teachers have the weight of the world on their shoulders. With all of the stress and pressure we experience it is greatly appreciated when parents go out of their way to be respectful, helpful, and positive.

• *Get both sides of the story.* About 90 percent of all problems between parents and teachers can be solved by giving each other a chance to tell their side of the story. Children will often give an account of what happened in a way that avoids placing any negative light on themselves, and this can lead to big misunderstandings. As a parent, it is hard not to believe every word your child says and to take his or her word for fact, but just remember that before becoming upset or displeased with a teacher you should give that individual the opportunity to tell the story from his perspective.

• *Be patient.* When I talk with my parents at the beginning of each year, I always ask them to be patient. I tell them how beginning a new school year with a new teacher and harder standards is difficult for children. Often they will complain that the work is too hard, that they are given too much homework, or that the teacher isn't fair. Sometimes when they say they don't like a new teacher, it really translates to the fact that they don't like having to do harder work than they did the year before. Good teachers find ways to smooth over this transition, but I ask my parents to bear with me for the first few weeks and to take any complaints from their child with a grain of salt.

• *Avoid negativity in the home.* There are times when parents will be upset with their child's teacher. It happens all the time, and even the most veteran, capable, and respected teachers will have times when parents are unhappy for one reason or another. When this happens, I would ask that parents deal directly with the teacher and avoid speaking about the matter in a negative way in front of their children. If a parent shows disrespect for the teacher at home, the child will feel that he or she has the right to show the same disrespect for the teacher in the classroom.

• *Give an occasional token of gratitude.* I love food, and some parents have sent their child into school with a container of soup or various cakes and desserts. It's so thoughtful, and it energizes me to continue working hard. Parents have also sent cards thanking me for my efforts. Such displays of gratitude mean a lot and really give teachers a shot in the arm. In our job, sometimes it is easy to become frustrated and depressed, and receiving such positive feedback from parents can really go a long way. Of course, I make sure to remain unbiased toward the child in the classroom. Parents shouldn't assume that being kind to the teacher will affect the child's treatment in class.

• *Contact teachers during appropriate times.* One of the most disrespectful things a parent can do is to show up at the classroom unexpected to have a discussion. I love to have parents visit the school, sit in during lessons, and talk with me about their child's performance. All of those things, however, should be scheduled. Teachers have enough on their plates, and when they are in the middle of a lesson they have worked extremely hard to prepare and all of the students are paying attention, it is distracting to have to go into the hall to talk with a parent who has shown up out of the blue.

• *Be a positive role model.* Whether on a field trip, volunteering, or just visiting the school, it is important for parents to realize that they are setting an example for all of the students. I once had a parent go on a field trip where we rode in a van for six hours. She sat in the passenger seat and talked to me using curse words the entire way. When she did so, she would lean over to me and say the expletives in a lower voice. The kids, however, could still hear every word. I was mortified. I had another parent show up to volunteer wearing a T-shirt that said in huge letters, "Don't Piss me Off." Things like that can be frustrating, but it is also just as bad when a parent shows negativity or favoritism, or doesn't treat the students with respect.

• *Handle issues with the teacher before going to the principal.* I can't say enough about this. Not only is it disrespectful, but it also isn't fair when parents contact the principal before discussing an issue with the teacher. If an attempt is made to handle the matter with the teacher and no progress is made, then a parent is more than welcome to set up a meeting with administration.

How Teachers Can Show Appreciation for Parents

Developing a good relationship with your students' parents is crucial to having a successful school year. When the parents know that you respect them and want to work closely with them in order to help their child, they are far more willing to help you in any way possible, whether it be by baking cookies, volunteering for a field trip, helping with homework, or dealing with disciplinary issues.

• *Contact parents often.* The number one mistake that a teacher can make is not keeping in contact with the parents. I can remember doing my student teaching in an eleventh-grade class. I was doing an assignment where I was supposed to familiarize myself with the student records, and I saw that Trent, the class clown who never paid much attention in school, had an IQ that was extremely high. I decided to call his mother to let her know I didn't feel he was living up to his potential in class. When I told her about the score on the test, she was shocked and said she never knew. She said I was the first high school teacher to ever even call the house and that my interest in the education of her son meant a lot to her. When Trent walked into the class the next day, he thanked me for the call and paid attention the entire lesson. He went on to have an A average for the entire time I was teaching, while he had only a D average previously.

That instance showed me a lot about the power of keeping in contact with parents, and I have made every attempt to keep the lines of communication open through cards, notes, phone calls, conferences, and home visits. Almost all parents will work with a teacher and bend over backward to help them if they are kept informed and notified about how their child is doing in class. This must be done, however, in a positive and respectful manner.

• *Give examples of ways they can help their child.* Parents always ask, "What can I do at home to help my child?" To make your life a lot easier, have an answer for them. I used to tell parents, "Just make sure he is reading or that you are reading with him each night." That was the main thing I asked of parents, and of course, that is essential. I started to learn, however, that when I was more specific with parents they were willing to really help implement my suggestions. I started asking parents to ask six key questions as they read with their child. I put these questions on a card and sent them home with each book:

After reading the title, what do you think this book is going to be about?

Why do you think the author chose to include this illustration?

What predictions can you make about what will happen next?

How did the story make you feel?

What did you think of the way the book ended?

In what ways did you enjoy this book?

Just by giving parents this guideline, it let them know the importance of not only making sure their children are reading the books but also that they are discussing what they read and putting some thought into the author's decisions. I began to use that strategy in all subjects. When we were doing fractions, I asked parents to buy flash cards and practice with their children. I soon started to notice sets of flash cards in kids' book bags, and when we went over fractions in class I could tell their parents had worked with them. When I would make copies of vocabulary worksheets, I would make five extra copies, and when parents wanted extra work, I would have them within arm's reach. I asked the parents to look over their child's writing each night to check for capitalization and spelling mistakes. I didn't want to just ask them to "check the grammar" because that can be too intimidating and overwhelming. Just checking the two items was reasonable. When I was in New York City and we were learning about dinosaurs, I sent home a letter encouraging parents to take their children to the Museum of Natural History. The following Monday a few students told me how they had seen each other there over the weekend. Not every parent is going to take a teacher's suggestions, but for those who will it is well worth it to give them guidelines of ways they can help.

There are so many things parents can do that have nothing to do with how much money they make, where they live, or how much education they received themselves. *Never assume that a parent won't give the effort.* What I have found is that parents will make the attempt if they are given specifics, and in the end that will take a lot of pressure and stress off the teacher and help the child be a lot more successful.

• *Thank parents for their help and support.* Parents can be extremely busy with work and the responsibilities of raising a family, and contributing to the school can really be time-consuming. When parents give their help, whether it be by tutoring in the class, making costumes for a play, or baking cupcakes, it is important to show them how much their efforts are appreciated. I would try to send notes home whenever possible, but usually because I was so busy I would only have time to give a call or thank the parents in person. The key is that in some way teachers let them know how much their help means to them and that their efforts are appreciated.

• *Remember the emotions involved with being a parent.* It is a difficult thing to turn your child over to someone else for seven hours a day. Parents put a great deal of trust in teachers, and when we teach their children we need to treat them with kindness and compassion just as we would like someone to treat our children. And when we talk with parents, we must find ways to discuss their child's progress in a way that is respectful and avoids being negative. It is also important to make sure that you are honest with parents. There is no need to blow smoke or try to dance around an issue. Parents appreciate the truth, but it should be told in a way that doesn't belittle or demean their child.

✎ Tips for Superintendents

Behaviors and attitudes tend to trickle down in school systems. If a superintendent is demanding and threatening, that will usually spread to the principals and then to the teachers. The students end up suffering in that environment. On the other hand, if a superintendent is positive and uplifting, that type of attitude will flow throughout the schools as well. The main thing for someone in such an important position to realize is that they should exhibit the type of characteristics they would want to see in those working with them.

• *VISIT THE SCHOOLS!* No matter who I have asked about the qualities of a good superintendent, this one comes up every time. For a person to really lead a school system, it just makes common sense that he or she should visit the schools often and get an up-close look at what is going on at each campus and within the classrooms. It means a lot to teachers, and they will use that, more than anything else, to judge the capabilities of a superintendent to lead well and make the best decisions for the school system. Surprisingly, visiting schools doesn't happen as often as one would think. I remember one year when the superintendent visited our school once, and another year when he visited twice, but never made it past the office. The teachers had all cleaned their rooms especially well and encouraged the students to be on their best behavior, yet he found no need to observe anything in the building beyond the confines of the principal's office. Teachers are very intelligent and aware of what is going on in a school system. They know how in tune the superintendent is with their needs, and they are highly aware of how much time he or she is spending within their schools.

• *Adhere to the chain of command.* If a parent comes to a superintendent with an issue dealing with a teacher, the first question should always be, "Have you discussed this with the principal?" If the answer is no, that should in almost all cases be the end of the conversation.

• *Give praise to teachers and principals.* Praise feels good. It makes us work harder and gives us a sense of accomplishment. I once had a superintendent walk up to me at a district meeting and congratulate me for my students' performance at the science fair. I had no idea she even knew who my students were, and it shocked me. I remember walking away thinking how she must really have her act together. Mrs. Jones called me one time to let me know how the superintendent had stuck his head in her classroom and told her that she should be extremely proud of her students' end-of-grade test scores. That small gesture meant so much, yet I wonder if he had any idea how those simple words would affect her.

Superintendents' responsibilities and duties are enormous, but by taking the time to visit the schools, respect principals and teachers, and give praise often and with sincerity, they will create an environment where everyone is working harder, the students are succeeding at a faster rate, and most of their problems will therefore be cut in half.

11. RESILIENCE

*The ultimate measure of a man is not where he
stands in moments of comfort, but where he stands at
times of challenge and controversy.*

—MARTIN LUTHER KING, JR. (1929–1968)

T HERE IS NO GREATER JOB in the world than raising
a child. It is also, unfortunately, one of the most difficult tasks anyone can ever undertake. As parents and teachers we must remember that when times are rough and
difficulties arise through the learning and growing process,
we have to stand strong and remain committed to doing
whatever is necessary to raise our children with optimism,
understanding, and love.

When Overenthusiasm Leads to Burnout

I love teaching, and I feel so fortunate to have the opportunity to work with students and hopefully make a difference

in their lives. It is truly a joy for me and a privilege, but there are times when it all just gets to be too much and teaching becomes mentally and physically draining. I can remember mornings lying in bed with the feeling that all the pressure and stress was so heavy that I couldn't even lift myself off the bed. The thought of dealing with the daily struggle, having to give 100 percent for eight straight hours, having to be totally prepared—on top of the fact that I hadn't graded those tests the students were waiting for and the principal mentioned she might be doing an observation today—was just too much. Teachers get burned out. I imagine it happens to us all. When you give so much of your time, energy, effort, and heart to any task, no doubt over time it will wear on any person and lead to a feeling of frustration.

How can we avoid burnout? There are several strategies I use that can be effective. First, I remember that sometimes we have to focus on the trees instead of the forest. At times I get upset that many children lack attention and that there are so many problems in education. When I start to focus on that, it usually gets me more frustrated, leaving me feeling negative about the possibility of "saving them all." When I get to that point, I just focus on the individual students in my classroom and think about their successes and what I can do to help each of them. That is a much more manageable task.

The second thing I do is say "no." That is a difficult one for a lot of people, but sometimes we have to realize that by taking on too many duties, we are hurting our students and using time that would normally be devoted to them. One of my answers when I am asked to sit on another committee or handle another duty at school is "I am involved with a lot of projects with my kids that are taking up a lot of my time, and there is just no way I can help right now." And teachers shouldn't feel bad about saying that.

The third thing I do is just step back. Sometimes I have so much going on with committees, programs, clubs, plans, and trips—you name it—that I just have to let it all stand still. I have to step away and take a few days for myself. Instead of getting to work early, I get to work ten minutes before the students. I plan lessons that require the least amount of effort, and when the kids leave, I leave. I have to do that for a few days in order to "rejuice." It doesn't happen often, but when I feel it is all getting to me and there is too much pressure on my shoulders, I allow myself to take a break, and I won't let myself feel guilty about it. In the long run I will be a much better teacher if I pace myself. It's like trying to win a NASCAR race. If you just drive and drive and drive and drive, you will eventually run out of gas, break down, or crash. You have to make pit stops along the way to refuel if you want to finish the race. In teaching, if you want to make it to the end of the year, and especially if you want to make teaching a lifelong profession, you have to rest along the way.

✎ When Others Don't Support
Your Enthusiasm

I mentioned earlier how each year I gave my class the assignment of learning all their presidents in order from memory. As part of the process I divided the class into groups and added one faculty member to each team. Every team who had all its members say all forty-two presidents without missing one would get to go to the big pizza party. All the students worked hard to learn their presidents, and the faculty member on each team worked hard to encourage the students and learn the presidents as well. Actually, they all worked hard every year, with one exception. The first year of the project the vice principal, Mr. Wordsman, claimed he was extremely busy but that he would love to participate and that he would be prepared when the day came to say the presidents.

On the testing day, every student and faculty member said all the presidents in order, and we all cheered and celebrated. There was one final person who needed to recite them, and that was Mr. Wordsman. I sent one of his team members to get him, and he soon walked into the room, stood in front of the class, grinned from ear to ear, and said, "Kids, I am so proud of the effort you have put into this task. Now," he said with a huge grin, "have any of you actually been able to say more than ten presidents in a row?" All the students' hands flew into the air. He looked a little taken aback and asked, "Well, have any of you been able to say more than twenty presidents in a row?" Like lightning, every hand went in the air. As the color slowly faded from Mr. Wordsman's face, he asked, "Have any of you been able to say every president?" Again hands filled the air. I felt nervous for him as I watched him begin to name the presidents, seemingly struggling to reach the dark corners of his mind to find the names. And then it happened: "John Quincy Adams, ah . . . now let me think. . . . Jefferson—no, wait. Jackson, no, Harrison." It was over. He had underestimated the students' abilities and he really hadn't prepared. He couldn't even get out of the top ten. The looks on the students' faces were of shock, and his teammates were appalled; because of him they wouldn't be able to go to the pizza party. I explained to the class that Mr. Wordsman was extremely busy and that his teammates should have made a greater effort to talk with him and make sure he knew that they had learned all their presidents and that it was crucial for him to know them as well. I actually felt embarrassed and so sorry for Mr. Wordsman.

The next day those feelings seemed to change when I was called into Mr. Wordsman's office. I expected him to apologize for ruining the class's perfect record, but instead he tossed the huge standard course of study book on the desk in front of me and said in a condescending tone, "Mr. Clark, show me where it says in the standard course of study that every fifth grade child must recite the presidents from memory." My mouth dropped open. He was right; it wasn't anywhere in our educational requirements for fifth grade. I tried to explain my rationale and how it really helps the students grasp American history, but nonetheless I had to sit there for thirty minutes listening to how important it was not to waste time and to closely follow the content outlined by the state.

I felt humiliated, and every time Mr. Wordsman walked by my room and looked in, I felt as if he was checking to see just exactly what I was doing in there. It is a horrible feeling to be questioned and doubted. I was working hard, and having those students learn those presidents worked and made a difference, but he didn't see it. He had been embarrassed, and therefore I was being punished. I remember my co-teacher Barbara Jones telling me, "Mr. Clark, stop worrying about it, or you are going to make yourself sick. Just focus on those kids and how well they are doing and how good they feel about themselves." So that is what I did. I put all my energy and focus into the kids. I shut my door and gave all my attention to my lessons. In addition, I made sure that I was using the standard course of study. Saying the presidents was a great idea in my mind, but I still needed to make sure I was covering every single thing that was required of my students. That way when I did require something extra, such as reciting presidents, I would be able to justify it by showing Mr. Wordsman, or whoever else doubted me, that all my bases were covered and that I was providing the students with what was required by our state.

Dealing with Intractable Supervisors and Principals

Principals have an incredibly difficult job, and I think it is hard at times to realize all the responsibility and pressure they are under. Problems are always springing up around a school, and no matter where they begin, they usually end up in the principal's lap. With all they are dealing with—budgets, parental concerns, hiring teachers, observations, staff meetings, disciplinary issues—it is easy to find fault when a principal isn't devoting enough time and energy to certain areas. It is also easy to become upset with a principal when a decision is made that you don't approve of. But over the years I have learned that sometimes administrators have reasons for their decisions that they can't share with everyone, and sometimes we have to put our faith and trust in their judgment.

With that said, it is important to remember that in all professions you are going to find some exceptional individuals and some who aren't as efficient. Some schools are blessed with highly motivated principals who are dedicated to supporting the teachers, inspiring the students, and making the school environment the best possible. Some schools have principals who tend to be stubborn, who lack vision, and who are more concerned with being in charge than actually leading the school.

When I was teaching at one school, one of my colleagues was being observed by an administrator. During the lesson the administrator stood up and said, "Honey, you're boring me and the kids to death. Have a seat," and then proceeded to walk to the front of the room and teach the lesson. I have heard an administrator say, "I want to make this clear: This is not the students' school. This is not your school. This is *my* school." I have sat in a meeting with my co-teachers who were scared to death of what our administrator was going to say to us. We were all worried because a habit had been made of humiliating teachers by putting them on the spot, demanding lesson plans, and inquiring about how multicultural education and differentiated learning were being placed into all subjects. The problem was that no matter what the answer was to the demands, the teacher was always made to feel inadequate and embarrassed. It was a nightmare.

With a supportive principal it is wonderful, but with a principal who seems to be working against you, life can be near impossible. How are teachers supposed to follow their own true course and not get fired? How are teachers supposed to try new techniques and methods with a principal who doesn't approve? How can teachers feel comfortable and inspire students if they feel afraid and uncomfortable in the school setting? Those are all difficult questions to answer, and I have watched numerous teachers quit and leave the profession, claiming they will never return because of the negative influence of a principal. There are times when even I wanted to quit, and the only thing they kept me from doing so were the students.

For all new teachers and for all of those who are dealing with a difficult administration, I am sorry, and thank you for dealing not only with the challenges of your students but with the stressful environment as well.

Here are some tips that might help to make life easier:

Prove yourself • Whenever a teacher is new to a school, or whenever a school of veteran teachers receives a new principal, there is always a period where it is important to prove yourself. Sometimes it takes time, and sometimes a new teacher may have to fit into a system and stifle a bit of his or her creativity until respect has been earned. However, once principals see those three key signs (good scores, good discipline, and good parent support), they are far more willing to allow you to branch off and teach in a way that fits your style and personality.

Here are some tips for new teachers:

Fly under the radar • This is just being honest. If a teacher is in a situation with difficult leadership, sometimes it is best to go in the classroom, shut the door, and teach in the way that he or she knows is most successful without drawing too much attention.

I have met a lot of college students who are fired up to go into the classroom. They feel that they are going to go in there and change the world, and I love that attitude; however, when first entering a school, it isn't the best idea to go in and make waves. In most situations there are veteran teachers who have been there for years who like things the way they are. It is a bad plan to go in and ruffle feathers by trying to impart change too quickly. The best course of action is to observe what is going on, teach your heart out, and bide your time earning respect before starting to make changes to the school environment.

Turn to colleagues for help and support • If the principal of a school is difficult to deal with, the one good thing that usually comes from this is that it brings the teachers closer together. Sometimes it's good to just vent and share frustrations with others. More than likely everyone is experiencing the same types of feelings, and talking about it together can offer great comfort.

Offer honey to the bear • Sometimes, for the sake of the students, it is best to find a way to appease the administration. If a principal is big on sports, offer to work the concession stand. If she is big on testing, offer to do a workshop for teachers on raising test scores. If he likes displays of student work, have the biggest and best bulletin boards all over the room and outside in the hall. In order to gain trust and get the freedom to teach in the way you wish, sometimes it is necessary to find a way to get the principal on your side. It is a shame to have to do that, but it is worth it if it enables you to offer better programs and instruction to the students.

Focus on your students · The best way to handle a stressful situation at school is to focus on the students. They are the reason we are there. They are the inspiration, and making a difference in their lives should come before all else. When times are bad, teachers should remember that the work they are doing is changing lives, and in many cases they have more impact on the children in that classroom than any other person in their lives. Let them be your motivation and the reason that you are able to deal with all the other chaos and stress that comes within the school environment.

IN CLOSING . . .

OF ALL OF THE WONDERFUL qualities that are mentioned in this book, no word better personifies a teacher than the word *passion*. Passion is why teachers teach and why parents devote their lives to raising their children. It is the fire in our hearts and the determination in our minds to make a difference.

This year I have met many first-year teachers who have a light in their eyes, excitement in their voices, and a passion in their hearts to change the world. The beautiful thing is, changing the world *is* possible. One teacher really can make an impact that will inspire children and motivate them to touch the people they meet in their lives with compassion, appreciation, humor, and love. One teacher can spark a child to seek adventure, to have confidence, to take risks, and to truly try to make the same impact on others that was made on them.

I will never forget the passion of Mrs. Owens, the gentle kindness of Mrs. Clark, and the adventure of being a student in Mrs. Roach's class. I will never forget the lessons taught to me by my parents, their confidence in me, and their unconditional love. The influence of those individuals who I love and respect so much has molded me and made me who I am today. All children, whether they are our own or our students, can be influenced in the same way and we all *can* make an enormous difference in their lives. No aspirations are too high, no dream is too large, and no goal is out of reach when it comes to having hope for the future of all of our children. That is the power of being a teacher and the beauty of being a parent.

APPENDIX

 Field Trip Proposal

Page 1: This should look very professional. It should contain a title such as "Washington, D.C.—Here We Come!" and have pictures of various things, such as the Washington Monument, Capitol Building, and White House. Also, make sure it is in a nice clear folder.

Page 2: This should be a letter to the parents telling them about the trip and how it is going to tie into that year's curriculum. Also, hit the basics: who, what, when, why, where (you should list here the chaperones you have already asked).

Page 3: This is the "how," and it is very important. The very first question everyone is going to ask when you mention this trip is "How much is it going to cost, and where is the money coming from?" Make sure you decide that and have a thorough listing of all the costs. If you will need to rent a bus through a bus company, give the company a call and get a quote. Also call various hotels and get quotes from them as well. Always ask to speak to a manager and say you are comparing prices from different hotels. That usually helps to lower the price a bit. If you think your students' parents can afford the price, tell them how much they will need to pay. Set up three dates over the coming months where they can make their payments. If the parents cannot afford the trip, you need to decide on fund-raisers and list each one along with the date. Giving that advance warning will really boost the participation. You can't deny a student the right to go on a school-sponsored trip because the family doesn't have the money. Therefore, you have to be ready to have some fund-raisers in order to cover those students whose parents can't afford the trip.

Page 4: This page should have a brief itinerary of the trip, noting key places the students will visit each day. Under certain items, such as the Museum of Natural

History, I will list a few key artifacts that the students will find exciting and want to see. When preparing an itinerary, the main thing to consider is feeding the group. I have found that nothing ruins a trip quicker than hunger. A fed group will be a happy group; they will have more energy and will have a lot more patience.

Page 5: This is a question-and-answer page. Figure out what their first questions are going to be and give them the answers. When we took more than one hundred people to New York City, my co-teacher and I had a meeting with everyone to answer any questions, but there weren't any. Everyone said the packet pretty much answered every question they had. It's that type of professionalism that you want to have in your packet. When people see it, you want them to say, "I can tell this trip is extremely organized."

Page 6: This is a basic permission form. I give my parents three options:

____ I agree to allow my child to attend the trip.

____ I am interested in allowing my child to attend, but I need to think about it a bit further.

___ Thank you for the offer, but my child will not be able to attend the trip.

Signed: _____

I ask them to return the form within one week.

✎ Questions and Answers to Give Parents for Field Trips

Q. Can students take CD players and Game Boys?

A. I say yes. A bus full of kids playing games quietly is a lot better than if they all talk at the same time. I make a note, however, that if it's lost or stolen, there is nothing that can be done about it and that we are not responsible for any electronics brought on the trip.

Q. How much spending money does my child need?

A. I say never more than $30. I don't want a child showing up with $100 and making others feel bad. Some parents say they want their child to get souvenirs for the family, but I tell them it is better for their child to focus on the trip than worry about all the souvenirs he or she has to buy. Also mention that they should talk to their child about keeping money in a safe place.

Q. Who will my child room with?

A. If they are younger than high school, I tell them there will be one chaperone and three kids in each room. The chaperone sleeps with his son with two boys in the next bed, or a mother sleeps with her daughter and two girls. If a female wants to go with a son, I tell the parent that she will have to pay the extra cost of the room, because only the parent and the child can be in one room. I don't allow parents to be in the room with students of the opposite sex. I have just found it opens a can of worms. I also mention that I will ask the kids to list six kids they would like to room with and that I will try to pair them with some of the kids on their list. I tell the students that after the rooms are assigned, I don't want to hear one word of complaint from anyone whatsoever, and they get the picture.

Q. Can my child call home?

A. I tell parents they must send their child with a phone card and they can call home on that. There are usually a group of pay phones in the hotel lobby, and we all go down at one time and take turns making short calls.

Q. Can my child take a camera?

A. Yes, but again, we're not responsible for any electronics.

Q. Can relatives who live in the city we are visiting meet the group?

A. No, no, no, no, no. I can't say it enough. Do not under any circumstances allow that to happen. If you let it happen once, you can never say no again, and it can be a nightmare. I have heard that the child hasn't seen her grandmother in ten years and this is the only chance for her to see her before she dies and just about every other story you can imagine. The main point is, this is an educational experience and not a family reunion. Often we are going to a show or somewhere where tickets are required, and having an extra person doesn't fit into the plan. Also, it's never a good idea to invite any adult into your group if you aren't familiar with that person beforehand.

Q. Can a younger sibling go on the trip if the parents pay for his or her way?

A. No. Say that unfortunately due to trip limitations no one other than students in your class will be allowed on the trip.

Q. Are there any educational requirements that my child must meet before going on this trip?

A. I usually say, "I expect each student to put forth a great deal of effort in preparation for this trip." I leave it basic. I also ask the parents *never* to deny the child the right to go on a trip because they are causing problems at home or not doing their work sufficiently. They might not deserve to attend the trip, but allowing them to go is such a wonderful experience and could help to turn them around and get them on track. I never want my students to miss out on such good opportunities for them to learn and grow.

Q. My child has to take medication; can he take it on the trip?

A. This can be tricky. Depending on your state and the type of medication required, the parent might have to go on the trip to administer the medication, or you may have to have a certified nurse. This isn't required with most medications, but in some states a child cannot be given Ritalin by anyone other than a parent or nurse. I ran into that problem one year, and it was settled by the child's just not taking the medication for six days straight. At the end of the trip I was the one who needed medication.

As an answer to this question, check with your school system. I tell my parents that they will be given a medical form to fill out. This contains all medication the child has to take daily, and it also asks them to list any medication, such as Tylenol, that the child can take for headaches or other problems. All medication listed must be placed in a zippered bag and turned in to a designated chaperone before we leave. That way no medication is left in the hands of the students. That chaperone is responsible for administering all medication. That form also lists medical conditions, social security number, insurance information, and emergency contact numbers. These forms are photocopied and put in three folders. One is left on my desk at school, and I give the others to two different chaperones to hold during the trip. I never want to take the chance of losing a folder and not having the information.

Having answers to common questions like the above beforehand will save a lot of time and energy in the long run.

✎ Website Recommendations

Lifetouch

Any teachers or parents interested in producing a book of memories for children can go to *www.lifetouch.com* for more information. A teacher might decide to do it for a classroom, or a group of parents might decide to do it for a school club, a church youth group, or some other type of group. This is the company I used each year to produce my students' yearbooks. It isn't cheap, but they will provide you with a very professional, long-lasting bound book of memories.

North Carolina Teaching Fellows

I never wanted to become a teacher, but when I was in high school I heard of a wonderful scholarship program that would pay for all of my college expenses if I agreed to teach in North Carolina for four years after I graduated. I took the scholarship because of need, *not* because of a desire to teach. Through a strange course of events, I ended up in the classroom, and I fell in love with it. It is because of the North Carolina Teaching Fellows program that I ended up teaching, and it is also because of the program that I was prepared once I stepped into the classroom. It is a phenomenally successful program, and I am eternally grateful.

Educators across the country have asked me for more information on the Teaching Fellows Scholarship. Many have expressed interest in beginning such a program in their states.

For more information, you can visit *www.teaching fellows.org*

The program is run by three of the most outstanding individuals I have met in my life: Gladys Graves, Jo Ann Norris, and Danny Bland.

Great Math Sites for Teachers and Parents

The best math site on the Web is *www.aaamath.com*. It is easy to use, and it covers all ages, levels, and topics. Every teacher who has access to a computer room needs to have every child using this program. The beauty of it is that every child can work on his or her own level, and the teacher can easily monitor the progress by glancing at the screen. Parents can also put their kids on the site. It serves as an instant tutor and offers great practice and review. Best of all, it's a free site!

Another good math site is *www.gamequarium.com*. This site is very similar to aaamath.com, but it is more colorful and is probably better for children six and under.

Great Education Site

A great site for teachers is *www.education-world.com*. It offers information on lesson plans, school issues, professional development, technology integration, and current events. It offers great resources, and it is updated frequently.

No More Kickball—Best Physical Education Site

Many students will say that kickball is their favorite sport to play in P.E., but there is such a thing as too much kickball. Just as the classroom environment needs to be full of varying programs, teaching styles, and activities, the physical education experience should be just as wide-ranging.

A great site that provides hundreds of different ideas and suggestions for P.E. is *www.pecentral.org*. It offers tips for every age, from preschool to twelfth grade. It also contains professional development information, assessment guides, and various resources.

College Information

Of all the things I have seen this year, one thing that has bothered me a great deal is seeing high school students who aren't being encouraged to attend college. That path may not be for everyone and it is possible to be successful without a college degree, but it certainly does help to have one. In addition, the college experience helps to make students more well rounded and provides them with limitless opportunities. I encourage all parents and teachers (not only the counselors) to talk with students and help them find the information they need about attending a university.

As always, one of the main things students need is someone to lift them up and show them that others believe in them. Many of our students already feel defeated and like they have no hope. One of the reasons so many high school students don't try is because they don't see a reason to. If students were told about financial aid, grants, and work-study programs, and if they knew that going to college was a reality, perhaps that would give them the impetus to focus, try harder, and make an attempt to become a better student.

One really good site for parents, teachers, and students to learn about colleges, financial aid, and the SAT and ACT tests is *www.collegeboard.com*.

"The Presidents Rap"

Music moves all of us. It lifts us up, gets us excited and puts a smile on our faces. I take every opportunity to bring music into the classroom, whether it is by playing classical music during tests, using music during games, or changing the words to popular songs so that it applies to our lessons. The students absolutely love it, and they are always singing them together before and after school, at recess, and on the bus.

Here are the words to "The Presidents Rap," which I wrote for my classes. If you would like to obtain the music that goes along with it, you can visit *www.ronclark.info* for information on obtaining a CD of this song, along with other educational songs I wrote for my students.

Now let's get down to some presidential learning
We'll start with George Washington straight from
   Mount Vernon
The first president and Commander-in-Chief
Fought the Revolutionary War so we could be free
John Adams was second, Thomas Jefferson third
When we fought for independence, their voices
   were heard (saying)
When in the course of human events (okay)
We took a stand and we've been doing it since (okay)
Pledged our lives and our fortunes and all
Defended our sacred honor for a better tomorrow

During the War of 1812 James Madison led

Again against the British and defeated the Red

Next came Monroe, then John Adams' son

Followed by Old Hickory, Andrew Jackson

Martin Van Buren was president eight

William Harrison was ninth (he only served 30 days!)

Number ten came Tyler, eleven was Polk

Then Zachary Taylor, Old Rough and Ready to Go

After Fillmore, Pierce and Buchanan were gone

Abraham Lincoln said that "slavery's wrong!"

And all through the Civil War he united the nation

And signed the Emancipation Proclamation

It's a tribute

To the Leaders of the USA

It's the Presidents Rap

All right, All right   Okay, Okay (He's the
   Commander-in-Chief)

It's a tribute

To the Leaders of the USA

It's the Presidents Rap

All right, All right   Okay, Okay

Andrew Johnson bought Alaska from Russia officially

And General Grant led the North to victory

Rutherford B. Hayes was number nineteen

The first president to get a telephone ring
Garfield was number twenty, Chester Arthur
   twenty-one
Followed by Grover Cleveland and Benjamin
   Harrison
But Cleveland wasn't done his aggression was firm
Re-elected and served two non-consecutive terms
Twenty-five was McKinley, Roosevelt twenty-six
The youngest president ever, and then it switched
To William Howard Taft, then Woodrow Wilson
The leader of our nation during WWI
After him Warren Harding, then Calvin Coolidge
The stock market crashed during Herbert Hoover
Till Franklin D. Roosevelt came and gave some
   hope and help
A New Deal was born, and all around relief was felt
He stopped the Great Depression, served for four terms
Till WWII, then it became Truman's turn
To finish off the fight and our rise to power
And pave the way for Mr. Eisenhower
President thirty-five The Great J.F.K.
Had a vision for moon walking till they took
   him away
We miss the King of Camelot and we cherish the
   memory
There will never be another John F. Kennedy
Thirty-six was Lyndon B., thirty-seven Nixon

Scandals and Contradictions, Disgracing Traditions

Screaming "I am not a crook,"

Resigned before impeachment, that got him off
the hook

After the crimes of Watergate Gerald Ford was
thirty-eight

Followed by Jimmy Carter who is from the Peach State

Ronald Reagan was the fortieth

Who was an actor first, and then the world became
his audience

(now check it out) Then his VP George Bush became
the man

During Desert Storm to stop Saddam was the plan

Clinton was forty-second, the economy was great

This country had the lowest unemployment rate

When Bush, Jr. came in office he dealt with
the attacks

Of 9-11 and the War with Iraq

Now after hearing this, isn't it evident that

Every one of these men deserves a president rap

It's a tribute

To the Leaders of the USA

It's the Presidents Rap

All right, All right   Okay, Okay (He's the
Commander-in-Chief)

It's a tribute
To the leaders of the USA
It's the Presidents Rap
All right, All right   Okay, Okay

"The States Rap"

There was once a popular song called "Thong Song."
Needless to say, it was not a church hymn, and it bothered
me to hear the students always singing it. We were learning
the states and capitals in class, so I decided to change the
words of the song to apply to geography. I bought the
instrumental version of the song and wrote out new words.
The next day I taught it to the class, and they were thrilled.
On our geography exam, every single student made an A.
People have asked for the words, and so I decided to include them. It really doesn't work unless you have the
background music and are familiar with the original song,
but here goes:

Geography is so good to us
We practice and we learn so much
We study that map from front to back
Get on the ball now don't be slack, uh
We like to learn about a lot
Of places that are cool and hot

We study every single spot
From Spain to South Dakota

And we plot those maps, maps, maps
And put them in a rap, rap, rap
Then it's a snap, snap, snap
Help me sing it again

And we find a place, place, place
Learn about the space, space, space
It doesn't take long
So help us sing our song

Annapolis, Maryland; Providence, Rhode Island;
Lincoln, Nebraska; Des Moines, Iowa;
Atlanta, Georgia; Tallahassee, Florida;
Montgomery, Alabama; Juneau, Alaska;
Phoenix, Arizona; Sacramento, California;
Carson City, Nevada; Richmond, Virginia;
Harrisburg, Pennsylvania; Baton Rouge, Louisiana;
Bismarck, North Dakota; Pierre, South Dakota;
Frankfort, Kentucky; Honolulu, Hawaii;
Topeka, Kansas; Springfield, Illinois;
Dover, Delaware; Nashville, Tennessee;
Columbia, South Carolina; Raleigh, North Carolina;
Helena, Montana; Jefferson City, Missouri;

Cheyenne, Wyoming; Madison, Wisconsin;

Jackson, Mississippi; Charleston, West Virginia;

Saint Paul, Minnesota; Olympia, Washington;

Lansing, Michigan; Boston, Massachusetts;

Montpelier, Vermont; Austin, Texas;

Concord, New Hampshire; Trenton, New Jersey;

Santa Fe, New Mexico; Columbus, Ohio;

Albany, New York; Salem, Oregon;

Oklahoma City, Oklahoma; Indianapolis, Indiana;

Augusta, Maine; Hartford, Connecticut;

Denver, Colorado; Boise, Idaho;

Salt Lake City, Utah; Little Rock, Arkansas

THANKS AND APPRECIATION

I would like to thank the following teachers, administrators, parents, and community leaders for their dedication, compassion, and tireless efforts to make a difference in the lives of others. These individuals are truly phenomenal.

Dixie McClain—School of Education, Lynchburg College, Lynchburg, VA

Christine Kane—Nubia Leadership Academy, San Diego, CA

Janet Franklin—Teacher, Beaumont Elementary, Knoxville, TN

Lisa Howse—West Central PTO, Rome, GA

Beth Campbell and Diane Bodner—Mark Twain Elementary, Bettendorf, Iowa

Barbara Coleman—Wingate Elementary, Wingate, NC

Barry Scott—Board member, Piggott School District

Marla Woolsey—Frontier Elementary School, Peoria, AZ

LaVern Watkins—Principal, Norcross Elementary School, Norcross, GA

Patty Thomas—Sedalia Park Elementary, Marietta, GA

J. Marie Johnson-Kola—Harrison School District Two, Colorado Springs, CO

Bob Bartoletti—Director of Professional Development, The College of New Jersey

LouAnn Durfey—Junior League of Jackson, Ridgeland, MS

Renda Rinestine—Director, Teacher Center at Eastfield, TX

Randall Holt—College student, determined beyond words, Lawrence, KS

Linda Farley—The Best School Cook in America—Thorton Elementary, Newton, NC

The entire Faculty and Staff—Burnet Consolidated Schools, Burnet, TX

In addition, I would like to thank all of my family and friends for standing by me this year and giving me support. I love all of you and can never thank you enough for the way you have touched my life.

Linda Dunlap—The Queen of Paradise. You are one of the most passionate and devoted individuals I have ever met. Keep making dreams come true at Wake Forest!

Elic Senter—Thank you for the high school perspective, the support, and the humor. Keep spreading your energy, your joy, and your love of life.

Kim Steward—What a pleasure it is to have you in my life. I have never met anyone who matches your wit, your cleverness, or your unconditional support.

Frances Castillo—You are the best administrator I have ever known. Thank you for fighting for all of the students at PS 83 and for providing a sense of support, admiration, and hope.

Mary Ellen O'Neill—You are a genius. You have given me more guidance and strength this year than anyone else in my life. I can never thank you enough for your calm understanding, your clear view of the world, and your honesty.

Richard Abate—You have my respect for life. You are amazing! It has been wonderful to work with you, but it has been even better having you as a friend.

Cindy Skaff—I can't imagine how I got so lucky to have you as a friend and colleague. You are the best "point guard" around; without you I would fall apart. I know if I call you and ask for the moon that I better go ahead and make plans for storage. I have no idea how you do it, but you always make the impossible happen, and I am forever grateful.

Howard, Brenda, and Adam—Thank you for fighting the good fight and for sharing the passion. I consider you all close friends and I appreciate all you have done for me.

Joey—Thanks for always being there. Your strength has been an inspiration for me this year. I'm proud of you.

Amanda, Bri, Erica, Ryan, Tiffany, and Crystal—Thank you for loving me enough to let me drag you into the woods for Survivor and for always being there when I need you. The walls of Fleming Hall would be proud to see us today. Amanda, thank you for the "Phil-payback" and for being positive. Tiffany, thanks for being on "red alert" for over a year now. Your help goes beyond words.

Barb—As always, you are my rock. I admire you so much and appreciate your friendship and support with all my heart. You remain the best teacher I have ever known.

Mom & Dad—To my A+ parents. Thank you for always showing me how to laugh and deal with life. Even when I call in the middle of the night, you act like you are awake anyway and you ask me what I need. You are always there, so loving, supportive, and patient. No son could have more love for his parents.

Tassie and Keith—What amazing parents you have become. I am so proud of both of you for raising Austin with such manners, respect, and compassion for others.

Austin—Mr. Entertainer. Mr. Suave. Mr. Muscle Man. You are one special, unique, and amazing young man, and I am so proud to be your uncle. Your energy and love for life will take you far. I love you, little buddy.

And to my "Adventurous Team"—**Barbara Jones, Joe Hooker, Faith Simmons, Amanda Nixon, Bri Arturo Bartelt, Fran Gary, Val McCabe, Kenneth Adams, Teviin Simmons, Brandon Shepard, Brian Tripp, Dentonio Grimes, Marina Bonner, Lee Anne Hooker, Kennedy KJ Reddick, Daniel Moore, Derrick Dunn, Julius Coles, EJ Patrick, Rubina Abdul, Tamara Lauriano, Quameisha Davis, Alize Beal**

Thank you for having the courage to go along on such an enormous journey. Life will never be the same.